THERE WAS A LITTLE GIRL

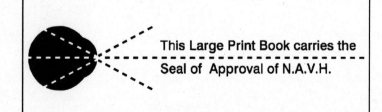

This Large Print Book carries the
Seal of Approval of N.A.V.H.

THERE WAS A LITTLE GIRL

THE REAL STORY OF MY MOTHER AND ME

BROOKE SHIELDS

THORNDIKE PRESS
A part of Gale, Cengage Learning

GALE
CENGAGE Learning·

Farmington Hills, Mich • San Francisco • New York • Waterville, Maine
Meriden, Conn • Mason, Ohio • Chicago

GALE
CENGAGE Learning®

LIBRARY OF CONGRESS CATALOGING-IN-PUBLICATION DATA

Shields, Brooke, 1965–
    There was a little girl : the real story of my mother and me / by Brooke Shields. — Large print edition.
        pages ; cm. — (Thorndike Press large print nonfiction)
        ISBN 978-1-4104-7664-7 (hardcover) — ISBN 1-4104-7664-2 (hardcover)
        1. Shields, Brooke, 1965– 2. Shields, Teri, 1933-2012. 3. Mothers and daughters—United States—Biography. 4. Actors—United States—Biography. 5. Models (Persons)—United States—Biography. 6. Large type books. I. Title.
PN2287.S37195A3 2015b
791.4302'8092—dc23
[B]   2014042043

Published in 2015 by arrangement with Dutton, a member of Penguin Group (USA) LLC, a Penguin Random House Company

Printed in the United States of America
1 2 3 4 5 6 7 19 18 17 16 15

CONTENTS

5

— Brooke Shields's baby photo album, 1965

There was a little girl,
And she had a little curl
Right in the middle of her forehead.
When she was good
She was very, very good,
And when she was bad she was horrid.
  — Henry Wadsworth Longfellow

INTRODUCTION

I'm told that even decorated soldiers' last words are often calling for "Mommy."

That is the first feeling that washed over me.

And on November 5, 2012, six days after I watched my mother die right in front of me, I opened up the *New York Times* obituaries and the feeling hit again . . . but it came with a wave of anger. I was so hurt my vision blurred. I couldn't believe what I'd just read, and I asked myself: How could I have been so stupid and so naïve? How could I have let my guard down? How could they have done this to my mommy?

Days earlier, I'd written my own simple and rather short obituary about my mom and had sent in the required $1,500. The following afternoon I got a call from the *Times* saying they wanted to print it on the front page of the obituary section. I said they could position it wherever they wanted.

They explained that they thought Mom deserved to have a more prominent placement. This made me feel like maybe after all these years, Mom would finally get some modicum of respect. And deep down we all want to know our moms deserve respect, don't we? The *Times* added that they didn't want me to pay the $1,500, but I explained that I was fine paying and thanked them for the offer. Suddenly the person on the other end of the phone stated that the obituary was, in fact, already being moved to a more prominent part of the paper, so a bit more copy would be needed. This was the first red flag.

"I am not giving an interview. Publish my written obit, please."

"Well, we may just need one or two additional facts that you could clarify."

"Listen, I submitted my personally written obituary about my mother and I sent in a check. Thank you."

"OK, we don't want to upset you. . . . How about we just take your obit and print that but add one or two additional facts about her upbringing and the like?"

"Fine."

They indeed called and asked one question about her deceased brother and if she had lived in any other city in New Jersey before moving to New York City. It was a two-minute phone call and it seemed fine. I was satisfied.

A few days later, on the stoop of my apartment, I was shocked and horrified to read a piece I'd known nothing about. It was a scathing, judgmental critique of my mother's life. I gasped and stared, wide-eyed, at the nasty, venomous piece of so-called journalism.

The first line read, "Teri Shields, who began promoting her daughter, Brooke, as a child model and actress when she was an infant and allowed her to be cast as a child prostitute . . . died on Wednesday." What an opener!

The obituary's author highlighted — completely out of context — the most salacious facts and quotes. He painted her as a desperate single mom who sold her daughter into prostitution and nudity for her own profit. He even distorted Mom's most famous quote, mistaking her wry humor for deep abuse — "Fortunately, Brooke was at an age where she couldn't talk back." This quote referred to the fact I'd been eleven months old when I shot my first ad, for Ivory soap, not to human trafficking of a minor into the sex trade.

Who the fuck did this guy think he was to write about a woman he never knew? How could he hurl such vicious allegations when an obit was supposed to be fact based? The piece was shocking and of the lowest common denominator, which was especially terrible coming from somebody who called himself a reputable journalist.

Reading the obit, I felt myself beginning to lose it. I started to take deep breaths, trying not to panic or pass out. I ran into the kitchen and began pacing around the table as I sobbed and rambled: Why are they so cruel? Why can't they let her be? Why can't they let her die without being nasty? Why can't they be kind to her just once? Why was it so easy and acceptable for him to degrade her? Where was the human decency? Someone's mother just died.

I walked in circles, crying and choking on my tears, and then left the kitchen and walked up the stairs to my bedroom. I bawled my eyes out and ranted for only a few minutes longer. Then I began to sense the rage. It was like a hot liquid traveling up my legs and all the way to my cheeks and actually radiating from my face.

The anger was terrible, but then I took a step back mentally and thought: Who is this guy? What is it about his own life and parental dynamic that caused him to write with such ignorance and venom? Why the drive to assassinate the character of a woman of whom he had no personal recollection, and whose path he had never crossed? What did she symbolize to him?

If this dead seventy-nine-year-old woman could elicit such a vehement response and vicious reaction so many years after her prominence in the public eye had faded — never mind that a man who had never been a mother or a daughter penned it — there was something there that needed to be explored. The relationships between mothers and their daughters are often fraught and fascinatingly complicated. I knew mine was. But what did she trigger in him? Why did he care?

Almost immediately, I knew what I wanted to do. It was time to tell our story — my mother's and my own. The story of my mother's trajectory through her life and through mine. The story of how I became who I am because of all she was.

This book is about everything that went into being Teri Shields. It is not a *Mommie Dearest* tale. But I'm not holding her up on a pedestal, either. There has been so much written about my mom, and most of it has been quite negative. This is by no means an attempt to idealize her or condemn her. It is simply my turn to tell the story as I saw and felt it. It's about the forty-eight years that I knew — yet never really knew — my mother.

My life — those forty-eight years of it — always existed somehow in relation to hers. She affected everything in my life. She was at the apex of it all. Nearly everything I did was for her, in response to her, because of her, or in spite of her. I was either emulating her or trying to define my independence from her. I was either trying to escape her or crash into her.

I thought about her all the time. She was part of my every day. Even though I worked hard and succeeded at creating a healthy private life and home with my grounded husband and beloved daughters, as long as she was alive, Mom's needs were never far away.

I remained preoccupied by her until she passed away. And afterward as well, obviously, because I am writing about her every day.

As a child, I literally couldn't imagine life without her. I used to think that if Mom died, I'd die, too.

Now I'm still here, with two daughters of

my own, and this book is about understanding what came before, and what comes next.

■ ■ ■ ■

PART ONE

■ ■ ■ ■

My feelings about my mother and about
our relationship are so confused that to
write them down with clarity would mean I
had them all figured out, which I do not.

— *Brooke Shields's diary*

Chapter One:
Teri Terrific

Who was my mother? I believe that I knew her better than anybody else did. And I didn't know her at all. I could wax philosophical and venture to say that my mother never fully knew herself, and that the persona she created became her reality. She saw herself the way she wanted others to see her and built up the necessary barricades between her real character and what she presented. She made it impossible for even her daughter to chisel past the myth.

For years, I thought she was the strongest, most honest and forthright woman ever. Looking back, I see that she was the most truthful white liar I will ever know.

I understand a great deal about my mother and about her complex nature, but there were facts hidden, brushed over, and manipulated. There was information lost in translation and lost to booze. And there was much sadness and pain and deep insecurity.

I have always felt that to really know another person, it requires a certain willingness to be vulnerable. Vulnerability equaled weakness in my mother's eyes.

I have asked myself these questions: How well did I know Mom? How deeply do any of us really know our mothers? And how well do they really know us?

Ultimately, how much of who I am is my mother? Do I have to know her better to know myself?

Of course, there is a lot I do know. There are stories, the ones she told me and the ones I heard from others. And pictures — so many pictures! They tell a story all their own.

I know that my mother, Theresa Anna Lillian Schmon, was born in Newark, New Jersey, on August 11, 1933. She had an older brother and a younger sister, who was the apple of my mom's eye. Mom was a perfect example of a middle child. She overcame her low self-esteem by rebelling and being a trailblazer. I smile thinking of her as a sweet but tough little kid whose attitude and humor made her a survivor. I am proud of my mom as a little girl. But for the most part, when I think about what I know of my mom's childhood, I just feel sad.

Evidently her mother, also named Theresa, was forced to stop going to school at nine years old to become the primary caregiver of her three siblings. My grandmother's mother had passed away, and she became an instant mother to three kids. Later on, she lost her younger brother to a freak drowning accident in Newark. I can only imagine the guilt and anger that comes from losing a sibling at such a young age and while on your watch. While researching my genealogy at the Newark History Society, I found a microfiche document that reported that in addition to these children, my grandmother's father had an entirely different family he was supporting on the other side of town. I am not sure if my grandmother ever found out about her father's double life, but I have a feeling that all these circumstances of her own life had to take a toll. This must be where her hardened personality began to develop. My grandmother was always a cold person in my eyes and would often throw out barbs about Mom. She resented her for something, and I saw it when we visited. Grandma never credited my mother for the things she had given her but instead gave acknowledgment to her other daughter. I guess she resented my mom for leaving her instead of staying and caring for her forever. If I did something annoying when we were visiting, her idea of a perfect insult would be to say, "Ugh, you're just like your mother!"

I took this as a compliment and thanked her. She'd then scoff at me, saying I was a sarcastic brat. One day Grandma offered to show me her dentures. I sat on her lap and grabbed her front teeth with my thumb and index finger, and she told me to pull. I did and her teeth came out in my hands. I burst into tears and thought I had ripped her head apart by the jaw. She laughed hysterically.

Eventually, when my grandmother grew up, there was a light at the end of the tunnel. She met and married John Schmon. They had three children: Johnny, Louise, and my mother, Teri. My mother's name was originally spelled the same way as her mother's, but she was forced to change the spelling because there were too many other Terrys and Theresas in her grammar school class.

As a child, Mom was left on her own a great deal and learned to be quite independent. She was a very cute little brunette with huge, dark-brown eyes. In pictures her eyes always stood out because of how dark and round her pupils were. She was a sweet, silly, and popular little girl who had an honest sense of humor. In first grade the teacher once asked the class why they thought that their area of Newark was nicknamed the Ironbound section. Mom raised her hand and exclaimed that it was because they were so tough!

Mom's father drove a bus. Her mom got a job at a doughnut shop and was the one who filled the doughnuts with the cream and the jelly. She evidently ended up getting fired for filling the doughnuts with too much jelly. She had other jobs but was basically a stay-at-home mom. It was the Depression, and it wasn't uncommon for women to work various jobs in pastry shops and the like or to clean houses. Even my mother worked, cleaning houses in Newark starting at a very young age.

Mom told me that before Easter one year she really wanted a little chick she had seen in the window of a toy store. The chick cost only two cents, but her mom would not give her the money for something so frivolous. Mom told me she cleaned houses after school for two weeks straight to make the two cents. But by the time she got to the store to buy it for herself, it was closer to Easter and the price had been raised to

three cents. She never got the chick.

But she was always smart and ingenious. At about age seven, she did make a dollar by sending in an idea to a soap factory. Her idea was to layer in decals in the center of the soap to encourage kids to bathe. They couldn't see the next fun decal until they washed the layers of soap away. She sent in a handwritten note to the company, and they sent her back a thank-you and a one-dollar bill. She claimed the company went on to make the soap and make a great deal of money from her invention. Mom gave her mother the dollar.

She was imaginative and adventurous, too, and her inventive way of thinking ended up giving me confidence to think outside the box and trust that my thoughts were unique. Of course, she was also OK with causing a little trouble, even then. When she was a very little girl, probably around four or five, she would run away from home and sneak into the movie theatre by getting on her tippy-toes and craning her neck to declare to the ticket lady, "My mommy's in there." The lady would wave her on inside and never notice if she did or did not come back out. Once inside the safety of the un-air-conditioned theatre, Mom would settle into a seat in the middle row and get lost in the stories told on the big screen. This was around 1938, and according to my mother, it was in a time when movies played all day long and periodicals played in between the screenings. World news would be sandwiched in between movies like *The Adventures of Robin Hood, Holiday,* or *Bringing Up Baby.*

Whenever her mother finally discovered — usually four or five hours later — that she had run away, they knew where to find her. The theatre lights would suddenly blast on and uniformed policemen would burst in with Mom's mother and come to retrieve the runaway. The minute her mother would grab hold of her tiny arm, Mom would just point up at the screen and say, "Movin' pictures, movin' pictures!" Inevitably, Mom would get a whupin'.

All her life Mom simply loved movies. She would escape into the darkness of the theatre, and that's where she found her home. She told me she usually went alone, and inevitably some guy would try to be inappropriate with her. She claimed it got to the point where she would just scream out, *"Put that away!"* She said it happened once and three separate men jumped up to leave. Nothing derailed her love of the movin' pictures. She was enamored of the glamour of movies and the fantasies they created. They were her original escape. It was fitting, I guess, for her to raise a child who would end up an actress.

Mom never seemed close to her mother, but she worshipped her father. They shared a special bond and a similar sense of humor. They both had a willingness to be silly. And neither cared about looking bad. Since birth he'd had a hole through the cartilage in his nose, and he would put a pencil through it and make a funny face to make Mom laugh. He'd imitate Charlie Chaplin in the movie *The Gold Rush* by sticking forks in two separate buns so they looked like little shoes and making the little bread feet dance on a tabletop. He'd chime in singing, "Now this is *abundance*!"

But even though Mom seemed to have revered her dad, I never got the impression that he was warm or overtly affectionate. Years later, upon my mom's graduation from grammar school, he could muster up the sensitivity to write "Phooey" in her yearbook. I found it later and saw that Mom had asked only her father and one of her teachers to sign her book.

He worked hard to support his family during very difficult times. Even though I got the impression that my grandmother never cared for my mother and in fact even grew to resent her, to me it seemed that Mom did genuinely feel loved by her father.

Sadly, though, Mom's dad died of lung cancer shortly after the "Phooey" incident. She was fourteen years old and this would be her first real loss of love. Mom's hero was gone and her mother was left yet again with three children to raise on her own.

Mom was able to stay in school and met the first love of her life in high school. He was a nice Italian boy named Salvatore Piccarillo and they became high school sweethearts. Mom would tell me stories about how she felt a part of his family and how his grandmother taught her to take one step at a time in life and not rush things or "sweat the small stuff." She also taught my mother the importance of perseverance and progress. This little old Italian grandmother would place her fingers on the kitchen table, touching her pinky to her thumb. She would separate her pinky from her thumb and then slide her thumb to meet it. The back of her hand would arch up every time her thumb met her pinky, and as she continued, over the length of the table, it looked very much like a huge caterpillar slowly making its way to a place in the shade. She'd made it all the way to the end of the table by taking little steps.

Mom and her beau, Sal, spent all their time together, and they became the stand-out couple at their high school. I loved the idea that he was a football player, and I imagined them as prom king and queen. These seemed to be some of the better years of Mom's life in Newark. She was said to light up every room she entered. She was special in every way.

After she graduated, Mom got a job working at Krueger Brewing Company, on an assembly line as a capper. She modeled a bit and was also often called out of work for photo opportunities to show her beautiful gams or greet various men in uniform. They would pluck her from the grind of the factory job and she'd have an interesting experience and hours off. Just like Marilyn Monroe in the famous photo from *Yank* magazine, it was always my mom who they wanted to show off the product or be the mascot of a factory. She looked like she was imitating the famous Betty Grable pinup photo in the bathing suit. She wore only fire engine–red lipstick and always showed off her long, sexy legs. She was stunningly beautiful, and her laugh was infectious. She excelled at everything she tried, and she read people astutely. She knew she was somehow different from her peers and wasn't the type to want to settle down.

Soon my mother started setting her sights past Newark and across the Hudson River to the bright lights and more cosmopolitan Manhattan. She wanted more. She wanted a big, fabulous life, and I guess she felt Newark couldn't provide it. She showed no regrets in leaving anyone behind. I often wonder what her life would have been like if she'd stayed. It seems impossible that she would have been content.

Mom started to take the bus into New York City every day for work and eventually got a job at the famous Gaslight Café. Her salary was minimal, and she made the majority of her money in tips. She was a coat-check girl who met the regular customers with just a smile and a nod, as she was always horrible with names. Once, while introducing a boyfriend to her mother, she forgot her own mom's name. She mumbled something and then just kept repeating her boyfriend's first name, feeling relieved that she could at least access *somebody*'s name in this horrible moment.

Well, this inability to recall names plagued her forever, but particularly at the Gaslight, where remembering the clientele's names ensured a larger tip. To counterbalance her deficiency, Mom would take the coat, cock her head with a wink, and go to the coat-check closet to retrieve a number check in its place. In the back, Mom kept a small notepad log of characteristics of the customers or tidbits about their lives — things they had mentioned or she had overheard. For instance: This man had a kid going off to college, had a sick family member, or had spent a holiday in a certain place. She also made a note of tie color or hair color or physical characteristics. She'd write: "red hair with crooked nose: Bob" or "slick side part and black hair, smells of Old Spice:

Jack." For the ones with no name, she would simply bring the claim ticket to the man and in a flirty tone, hands on hips, say, "Now you, how come you're not wearing my favorite yellow tie? Shame on you! Next time I want to see it. Enjoy your evening."

The men all felt special and, with stoked egos, reached farther into their pockets for a tip.

Mom crumpled her cash tips and shoved them in her pockets. At the end of the night she'd take the bus back to Newark, and her mom would be waiting with the ironing board up and the iron hot and ready. Mom would dump out the balled-up money and give them to her mom, who stayed up ironing the bills until they were all flat and in a stack. I'm not sure my mother ever got to keep any of this cash for herself. I suspect it all went to her mother for the care of the family. Mom never seemed to resent this and instead began to clock the prospects of a bigger world, one that didn't involve a daily bus commute.

She began to grow away from Sal. They always remained friends (until the day she died), but she decided to go off on her own and move to New York City. She set out to get an apartment and was able to secure one with decent rent on the east side in the

Fifties. She then began working in the Garment District in various stockrooms and, sometimes, as a model. Mom continued to send her mother money when she could. I have found thank-you notes from my grandmother and my great-aunt Lil thanking Mom for the rent money.

My mother wanted a more upscale career but had no experience or education in sales or management. But she didn't see that as an obstacle. She often said to me growing up, "Brookie, where there's a will, there's a way. Don't take no for an answer and never let 'em see you sweat. Figure out what you want and find a way."

She applied and got a job at the makeup counter of the posh uptown department store Lord and Taylor. It would be here that she would meet her longtime friend and my eventual godmother, Lila Wisdom. Lila was from Tucson, Arizona, and was younger than Mom by a few years. They became the best of friends, but Mom always saw herself as the captain of the ship. I only knew my mom as the captain of the ship, so this made sense to me. Lila was from a small town and had graduated from college. Mom acted like her bossy big sister, and their dynamic worked.

Because Mom also had zero training in

the world of makeup beyond applying her ever-present fire engine–red lipstick and matching nails, she had to be creative and seemingly confident. Her job was to make up the customers and subsequently sell them products. Mom was right-handed and unable to use her left steadily or contort properly to use the brushes in her right hand to apply eye shadow and the like on both eyes. After creating a few Picasso-esque faces, she came up with a solution. She would do the left side of a woman's face with her right hand and then turn the woman to face the mirror, hand her the brush, and, like a wise teacher, say, "Now let's see if you can do what I just did to the other side of your face."

Women loved the attention and instruction and were empowered by learning a skill from the expert. They bought copious amounts of products, and everybody was happy. Management thought Mom was a genius, and she was soon promoted. Lila was Mom's boss in the beginning but soon Mom was practically running the place. It was a gift she had — how she could turn her weaknesses into seeming strengths. People looked up to her and thought she could do anything, even though she was technically not trained. She was a person who would never admit to not knowing something.

Mom was now meeting a more uptown crowd and soon had many new friends. She was exposed to the fabulous fifties in New York City and all it had to offer. Mom befriended many gay men who were hairdressers or in fashion, and she beguiled many members of the New York social set. Her usually brown-red hair was blond at this point. She was a five-foot-nine bombshell with a narrow waist; long, gorgeous legs; and a sexy hourglass figure. She seemed to celebrate her physique and had no issues wearing a bikini or minidress. She had a friend named Joanne who was a fellow blond. Joanne had a mean parrot that Mom taught to curse. Jo and Mom often wore one another's bathing suits and always took fun pictures on various boats and with various men suitors. The same leopard one-piece has shown up in many photos of Mom as well as Jo.

Mom loved to have her photo taken and always had a glimmer in her eye and a glass in her hand. In photos of her with other people, your eyes are always drawn directly to my stunningly beautiful mom. The men were either handsome or rich, and you could tell they wanted to shower her with

the good life — the life she so coveted.

One particular gay couple became Mom's closest friends. They had a place on Fire Island and often repeated the story of how one day Mom was walking one of their poodles on a leash on a boardwalk. The dog wrapped the leash around Mom's legs and she got totally tangled up and fell head over heels on the wood planks. Her dress flew up

over her head and she was wearing not a stitch of underwear.

Mom never parlayed her many talents into a profession but kept starting jobs, excelling in them by sheer street smarts and innovation, and moving on. She seemed to be searching for some kind of recognition or social status and an escape from her roots.

It wouldn't be long before Mom met a man to whom she became engaged. I never heard much about him and was shocked and saddened when I found out why they never actually got to take a walk down the aisle together. Mom told me the story of his death every time she took me to have a cheeseburger at P. J. Clarke's original Fifty-Fifth Street and Third Avenue location.

Turns out Mom and her fiancé, who I later learned was named Morton Gruber, were on a double date with a girlfriend of Mom's and her boyfriend. They all were in the car together on the way to have drinks and dinner at P. J. Clarke's. They were having trouble finding a parking spot and didn't want the ladies to have to walk far. Mom's fiancé was behind the wheel and suggested he drop the three passengers off at Clarke's to get a table. He would find a spot for the car and meet them inside. Mom and the other couple went in and waited the normal ten minutes for a table and sat to order a cocktail. Some more time passed, and the group began to discuss how bad parking had gotten lately. Even more time passed and they began to get a bit curious and even slightly concerned. Did her fiancé suddenly get cold feet? This joke ended up being a terrifying and morbid premonition. Moments later, sirens were heard and red lights flashed through the paned windows. Everybody rushed outside and was horrified by what they saw.

This was at a time in New York City when Third Avenue was a two-way street. Evidently, Morton had parked the car on the opposite side of Third Avenue from the restaurant and was crossing the street when he was hit by a car. His body was thrown thirty feet. He was dead on impact, and by the time the ambulance came his watch and wallet had been stolen. The whole story was shocking to me. I couldn't believe that people would steal off a dead or dying bloody man. And if he had lived, I would have never existed.

According to my mother, the next day Third Avenue was converted to a one-way street heading uptown. It turned out to be a bit later than the next day, but the day after sounded more dramatic and appealing to her. This was just another one of my mom's slightly lying truths.

I can only imagine the sense of loss my mother must have experienced. I believe that because she lost her dad as a kid and then her fiancé, a deep fear of abandonment began planting its roots in her heart. Mom was a tough cookie in many ways, and she did what she could to move forward. She was never one to talk about her true feelings but suffered inside and alone.

Her life continued and she found other

suitors but no proposals she wanted to accept. She wanted to date, have fun, be entertained, and, I am guessing, drink. She was the life of every party and I don't believe her drinking had done more at this point than help her maintain her fun-girl status. At one point Mom did meet another man with whom she was rumored to have been very serious. But it wasn't until years later that I would hear the truth about that relationship.

While she had plenty of tragedy in her life, she also had a great deal of fun. Mom loved Broadway and anyone associated with the theatre. Some years later she ended up dating a married (but separated) man named Murray Helwitz, who was treasurer of the Shubert Theatre. They dated for a while, and Mom fell right into the world of premieres and late-night cocktails, dinners, and dancing at various dinner clubs. Social hobnobbing like that made my mother come alive. She befriended all the local bartenders, coat-check girls, and restaurant managers. This seemed to be the beginning of a lifelong pattern where Mom gravitated toward those she called the underdogs.

While seeking her fabulous and glamorous future, she always seemed to hover on the fringe. It appeared she meant to inhabit two paradoxical worlds. It was an odd paradox because she wanted to be accepted into a more elevated social status, but she held tightly to a darker and more troubled socioeconomic echelon. She was seeking some kind of recognition and a level of improvement in her life but fought it at the same time. It seemed that she was longing for, craving, an escape from her roots. Yet she could never quite give them up. She'd revert to a tougher type of talk if she felt intimidated. I always said she wore being from Newark like a badge, flashing it when necessary or threatened. Whenever she felt a crack in her armor or felt a moment of social ineptitude, she'd counterbalance with a brash declaration of her Newark upbringing. She often outwardly credited Newark as the reason she couldn't be beat. I always loved visiting there with her because it felt uncomplicated. But I also loved leaving because I would get bored, just as she did.

The bartenders in particular seemed to look out for her. Once, while Murray and Mom were in a fight, a bartender spotted Murray with another woman, sitting at what had been "their" table. The bartender reached under the counter for the phone and called my mom. He quietly informed her that her beau was currently at the joint with another gal. Mom thanked him, took a quick shower, and put on the new mink coat Murray had purchased for her as a gift along with a pair of high heels. Decked out in *just* a fur and heels, Mom cabbed it to the restaurant, walked to the back of the place, stood in front of the table for two, and looked right at Murray but angled herself slightly more toward the other woman, who turned out to be his wife. Seems like they weren't so separated after all! She asked him if he liked her new fur coat. As she asked, she proceeded to open it up and do a full twirl before wrapping her naked self back up and continuing out the restaurant. On the street she may or may not have cried, but she had made a point. Mom liked to make such scenes, and her various dramatic antics would become legendary.

The fur-coat story aside, clothes paid an important role in my mom's life, and she chose them carefully. Early on, she recognized the power of certain labels. But she also realized she was unable to afford them. She knew how to dress for various social environments and would not let her lack of finances infringe on her wardrobe. In the late fifties and early sixties Emilio Pucci had become wildly popular. Mom loved the bright colors of Pucci and thought it ingenious how he wrote his name throughout the patterns. But she was unable to afford the famous print mini shift dresses all the uptown ladies were wearing. So Mom once again had to be creative.

And that she was. Mom bought some fabric in a print that was practically indiscernible from the now famous Pucci patterns and fashioned her own shift dress. She sewed it herself and then in pen she wrote her own name, "Teri," in cursive on all the same areas one would find the esteemed signature "Emilio." She recalled many socialites coming up to her at a cocktail party and commenting on the specialness of her dress. "I just love your Pucci, Teri!" Mom said she made a point of saying thank you and walking away so her secret stayed safe. She would joke that she was fine as long as she wasn't caught in the rain, because then if she had been unlucky enough, her dress would begin looking like a fashion by Rorschach test, with ink blots developing where her name had been previously so neatly placed.

Mom coveted the clothes she saw the rich women wear, and eventually learned to hunt them down in various Upper East Side thrift shops. She knew those were the places that the Park Avenue women were likely to deposit their old Gucci, Courrèges, or other designer labels. She combed through the racks and stacks and over time, and with her keen eye, was able to procure and savor a wardrobe that any proper Upper East Side WASP would deem appropriate.

It was thanks to this wardrobe and her recently, intently, avariciously learned rules of etiquette that Mom began dating more and more well-bred men and being invited into communities previously reserved for high society, for the educated, wealthy, and elite. Mom felt at ease and if she was at all insecure about her level of education, she made up for it with her humor, her style, and her astute ability to read a room. Mom's wry wit and her keen human observations made her a welcome dinner date or companion to anyone lucky enough to have her at their table. When you added alcohol to these characteristics, she was hard to resist. Her drinking at this point in her life, although probably necessary for her confidence, was still not a negative. Mom dated senators and theatre owners, bankers and trust-fund kids. She was wined and dined by them all. Mom began being recognized around town as the beautiful and vivacious

"Teri Terrific."

Mom looks happy in the photos I have from this time. I believe that during this period of her life, she might have actually been. There was no sadness in her eyes yet. This may have been the happiest I had ever seen her. She was on the ascent and having fun. She looked the best she had ever looked and was celebrated for all she wanted to be. I held on to the fantasy that one day I'd be able to help Mom return to that feeling in her life.

She seemed gorgeous, carefree, and very alive. She was living the life of a single woman in New York City in the early sixties. But she was getting a bit older according to the current social mores, and I believe she began wanting a bit more security and a more substantial relationship.

Well, such a relationship was around the corner, and although it may not have been what she had expected, it changed the entire course of her life.

CHAPTER TWO:
SHIELDS AND CO.

If asked, Mom always boasted that late '64 and '65 were a very good and very busy time. Over the course of a year my mother met my father, got pregnant, married my dad, had me, and got divorced.

As the story goes, Mom was nursing a broken heart at a local watering hole called Jimmy Weston's with an equally sad buddy who had just been dumped by his lady friend. His name was Jack Price and he evidently knew my father from around. Together Mom and Jack ventured out to commiserate and drown their sorrows. Evidently my twenty-four-year-old dad, still wet behind the ears and newly graduated from the University of Pennsylvania, walked into this particular bar on the Upper East Side by himself. He stood six foot seven with thick black hair slickly side-parted and combed over like a little boy's. His strong jaw and Roman nose gave his face a regal appearance — to me, his face always looked a bit like the Statue of Liberty's or like one of the Greek gods. According to my mother, Dad was wearing shined Belgian loafers, a crisp shirt, and a navy blazer. He was beautiful.

Mom claims she took one look at him and thought, *I want that!* Somehow introductions were made as they often are in these bars filled with regular customers. Friends of friends introduced everybody all around and Mom quickly devised a plan. She proceeded to focus on getting her drinking buddy hammered so as to unload him. Once Jack began to stammer, Mom made her move. She asked my father to help put her friend in a cab. She told the cab driver his address and then stood on the street with my dad, open to suggestions.

"Can you believe he just left me!" Dad offered to take her home.

Here she was, the five-nine blond beauty with legs like Cyd Charisse's, the attire of a well-bred New Yorker, and a riveting wit. These were her most beautiful years, and when you add in some inhibition-erasing cocktails, she became captivating. How could he resist? This was all I got of this part of the story, but evidently she went back with him to his apartment on East

Fiftieth Street and there it all began. My father missed his flight to Los Angeles the next day and had to make up a story to tell the girlfriend he had intended to visit. Mom claims they didn't leave the apartment for three days. I did not need to hear that particular detail, but I got the impression things went well. Mom and Dad began dating (and finding out about one another).

My dad came from a very, very different background from that of my Newark-born mom. His mother was Infanta (Donna) Marina Torlonia, an Italian-born aristocrat and daughter of the 4th Prince of Civitella-Cesi, Marino Torlonia, and Elsie Moore, his American wife. Marino had been the first private banker to the pope and was the primary administrator of Vatican finances. Mussolini even claimed one of his properties for his summer residence, paying him only one dollar.

Dad's Italian mother, Marina, married New York City–born tennis player Francis Xavier Alexander Shields. "Pop-Pop" or "Big Frank," as people referred to him, was president of the Davis Cup and a finalist at both Wimbledon and the US Open. (This was his second marriage.) Pop-Pop was also an actor under contract in the old studio system. It was said that his contract had

47

been used as collateral in a poker game and because of a loss he was forced to switch studios. Mom and I would see some of his movies later, particularly *Come and Get It,* which was directed by Howard Hawks and starred Pop-Pop and Frances Farmer.

My grandparents divorced after having my father, also named Frank, and his sister Marina. His mother then married Ed Slater, another American, and divorced him after having a son and daughter. Pop-Pop had two more children with his third wife, Goody Mortimer. It was always interesting to me that in almost every case, there was an aristocrat marrying outside the social boundaries, and to an (American) commoner. My royal grandmother married a tennis player–actor from New York City, my dad married a woman from Newark, and I first married a tennis player from Vegas. Dad would comment on this when I was about to marry Andre. (Clearly, none of the couplings ended well.)

A few years later it was said that my grandmother was in love with a married man. While on her way from the wedding of her nephew in Italy to the reception, she was killed in a horrible car crash. It was rumored that she purposely did not ride in the same car with her secret love so as not to create a scandal. The sad irony is that this man's son, Roffredo Gaitani Lovatelli, would die the same way. More grim, however, was that Dad's mom was decapitated and her only son, who was just eighteen years old, was forced to identify the body. In Italy, the firstborn son is considered the next of kin, and because she was divorced at the time, he had to fly over from the University of Pennsylvania, where he was a freshman, to Italy to identify the body.

It must have been a very sad time in my father's life. I don't think he was ever the same after his mom died. Even though he had been at boarding schools and often not with his mom, she was a prominent figure in his life. She lived the life of a royal and jetted all over Europe. Mom once claimed she saw postcards from Dad's mother from places like Gstaad, where she wrote she was sorry she could not be with him for Christmas but was skiing and would see him soon.

Like Dad's mother, my mom was tall and statuesque. His mother would be considered more of a "handsome" woman rather than the beauty my mother was, but they each had a strong presence. Marina was strong and obviously in control. Maybe my dad saw something of his mother in my mom? I'm sure he was drawn to her power and seeming confidence as well as her beauty. He did not seem to have any qualms about my mother's age. She was eight years older than he was and this was not common in the sixties. I guess he couldn't resist the gorgeous spitfire who made him laugh. However, Mom's upbringing and background would later be a prominent obstacle.

But at the time, even though she wasn't a college graduate or an upper-class society debutante, I'm sure Dad found Mom's charisma and humor refreshing. She was known for her energetic personality and game attitude. It appeared that she could converse with people from all walks of life and could blend into a variety of different social settings seamlessly. But he wouldn't have known at first that she was also quite volatile and frequently prone to drama in her relationships. He was no doubt going to be confronted with his own version of the fur-coat incident if he stayed around long enough.

Soon Mom discovered she was pregnant. When she told my dad, he must have felt a sense of panic — and rightfully so. He wasn't ready to be a father. He was just starting his life in business and was forced to travel a lot. He had less money than one would think, and he was still a baby himself.

Dad really did not know how to handle this. He must have told his dad, who took it upon himself to try to persuade my mother to terminate the pregnancy. I was told my grandfather called my mother to meet with him to discuss the situation. Mom met Pop-Pop at his apartment and he sat her down to talk. He requested that mom terminate the pregnancy, explaining that having a child out of wedlock would risk my father getting kicked off the Social Register.

Mom explained that she hadn't meant to corner my father into marrying her and would not hold him accountable for the child. Personally, I believe my mom really did want to be married to my dad but would never have purposely gotten pregnant to do so. She wanted a baby. Period. She craved unconditional love. Pop-Pop (rather hypocritically) alluded to the fact that because Mom and his son Frank came from such different social backgrounds and social status, it seemed an inappropriate coupling. Basically, it just wouldn't look good for my dad to father a child with somebody from Newark. He discreetly slid her an envelope and asked her to take care of the "situation."

According to my mother, she nodded in

agreement, explained that she fully understood the state of affairs, took the envelope, and departed. She had no intention of getting an abortion but saw no reason not to take the cash. Instead of going to a doctor, she proceeded immediately to a favorite antique store. There she used the money in the envelope to buy a cherrywood oval coffee table whose four sides folded up with brass brackets to form a sort of connected tray. She was not surprised or angry but defiant as always and knew she wanted the baby and that was that. It's funny — that table would become a favorite standing tool for me as I grew up. I remember teething on it and loving to repeatedly fold the sides up and down and up and down. The table saved my life and helped me to stand.

I didn't learn the truth until recently, but Mom, after buying her new coffee table, suddenly decided to play hard to get. She stopped talking to my father entirely. She said she didn't want anything from my dad but just wanted the baby. She refused to see or even speak to him. Mom was trying to get Dad to realize that he could not live without her. My father, distraught by the pregnancy, and afraid for his future, went to Mass (for the first and last time) and received communion the day he found out about the pregnancy. He was heartsick. He was evidently so in love with my mother that he sent her flowers galore and even sent my godmother, Lila, a cactus garden because she was from Arizona. As much in love with my mom as he was, my father was still not ready to get married or be a dad. He knew Mom would not terminate anything except their relationship, but he was extremely conflicted. Mom cut him off for a few months and hoped he would miss her enough to propose. She made it very clear to everyone that the baby was here to stay, and both my father and grandfather knew it.

When my mother originally told me this story, she had altered it entirely and decided to tell me that my father had left the country during this time. She claimed that when he returned and saw that she had not had an abortion, he proposed. She said that she just calmly waited for his return and enjoyed the life growing inside of her.

My mother's version of the story has my dad going away for a few months and eventually not being able to stay separated from her. Like a comic-book detective, she loved declaring, "Your dad couldn't stay away from me, and I knew he'd eventually come sniffin' around again."

Mom continued on with her altered story, adding that when Dad did return to rekindle, he was shocked to see her big belly and immediately demanded she marry him. Mom loved the dramatic addition of saying that Dad thought he'd return and she would be thin again and without child, but when he saw that she was hugely pregnant, wanted to be a family.

In her version of the story, she opened the door and he turned white as a sheet. "Jesus Christ, Teri. . . . I thought . . ." Not ever being one to be told what to do, Mom reveled in the idea that she could be so in control and shocking.

But the truth was Mom avoided him until he said he wanted to marry her. I guess she broke him down. He did love and miss her, even though he wasn't really ready for any of this. In the end, Mom happened to be desperately in love with my father. Once he claimed he wanted to get married, she ended his solitary confinement.

Dad bought a small diamond solitaire engagement ring from Tiffany (that would eventually be thrown out the seventh-floor window during a fight between my parents, but that's another story). And one day in April, Mom, dressed in a gray wool gabardine maternity dress, went with my father down to city hall. Dad had forgotten his ID at home and had to cab back to retrieve it. For years Mom made up a story that my father was so young — and looked so young compared to her — that the city-hall official was forced to ask for his ID, fearing he was underage.

Sadly, it was not until I wrote this part of the story that I realized this was another little white lie. He had forgotten to bring ID, but it had nothing to do with how young he looked. Everybody is required to have a form of ID when applying for a marriage license. Ah, over the years how implicitly I have believed even the most outrageous mini-lies that my mother has told me. I simply took these fun facts as actual fact when Mom was just envisioning the movie that she wanted to create. You tell stories over and over enough times, and in a way, they become the new reality.

When Mom spoke of this time in later years, it seemed as if she had no worries whatsoever. She was feeling great and was taking so many vitamins that they filled a shoe box. She recalled standing on a corner waiting for the light to turn green one day and her hair — which was usually thin and sparse — had become so healthy and thick that she could, for the first time in her life, feel it swaying in the wind. She enjoyed being pregnant and said she hardly had any morning sickness at all.

My parents moved to an apartment on East Fiftieth Street. I have only two pictures of my mom pregnant. In one Dad is lying on the couch and Mom is standing by a window holding a glass. This was probably the only photo of Mom holding a glass that did not have alcohol in it. Mom was extremely healthy while she was pregnant and I believe drank very little if at all. In the photo she is backlit and wearing a big yellow muumuu-like dress. She is smiling.

This time for my parents seems to have been a rather uneventful one. Mom prepped for the baby and Dad was working in New York City. In the other photo, they are at a restaurant where my dad is looking lovingly at my expectant mom, who is proudly displaying her diamond. They looked like such a beautiful and contented couple.

On May 31, 1965, my mother and father, along with my godmother, Lila, and a date, were on their way out of the city to watch the Indy 500 on a big-screen TV. The group stopped off at a diner to grab a bite to eat before the start of the race. Mom stood up to go to the ladies' room and suddenly her water broke. It was two months before my due date, and a wave of panic surged through my mother's veins. The only calm one in the place was the waitress who purportedly got immediately down on the floor and began mopping up the mess with her table rag. Mom would later remark at how nonchalant the woman was and how unfazed she was by what had just happened. By the time my dad got Mom to the New York Hospital–Cornell Medical Center maternity ward, she was in labor. Everybody was on high alert because of how premature I was. Mom said they gave her some medication, and from that moment on, she had no recollection of what took place. She awoke to my father leaning over her saying, "We have a perfectly formed baby girl."

Mom remembered thinking that Dad was a lucky bastard who always got exactly what he wanted — he had hoped for a girl and Mom had prayed for a boy. I never got to understand why my mother wanted a son over a daughter. I could speculate as to the psychology of losing her father, or having a less-than-stellar relationship with her mother, but for some reason Mom wanted a boy. She had picked out the name John and was *sure* I was going to be a boy. However, it was days before Mom got to see her perfectly formed baby girl because I had been whisked off to the nursery and placed in an incubator to be monitored. Days passed and still Mom had not laid eyes on me. She began getting suspicious as to why her baby was being kept away from her. She started experiencing late-night paranoia that it was all a lie and that there was actually no baby. She feared the baby had died and people were not telling her the truth. I would not learn until much later why Mom had such a fear of me dying. The doctors reassured her she had a healthy five-pound, three-ounce daughter who was safely tucked in her incubator, and they encouraged Mom to rest.

Mom desperately tried to sleep through the next lonely night but claimed an annoyingly squeaky door kept her awake. She summoned a nurse to request that the door be oiled so she could rest. The attending nurse looked right at my mother, with slight annoyance in her voice, and explained that the "squeaky door" was in fact Mom's newborn baby in the nursery next door, and nothing they could do would stop it.

Mom waited in silence after the nurse departed and, with mounting desperation, hobbled off her hospital bed and snuck out of her room. She was not convinced that any of these stories about her infant were true, and with increasing hysteria, she was determined to find out the truth. She snuck into the nursery and began frantically looking for her daughter's name on the cribs. Her fear and confusion became fueled by the fact that the manufacturing company of all incubators and cribs at that time was called Shields and Company. She went from thinking she had no baby to seeing every single crib with her baby's name on it. It must have been surreal.

Mom looked to the far end of the nursery and saw two cribs at the back a bit apart from the others. One crib was faced out and the other was faced to the wall. It was an unusually busy time for birthing babies and space was tight. In those days the children being placed up for adoption were put in cribs and then turned away from the glass so the birth mothers couldn't see the babies. It was thought to make the transition less fraught for the mother. It just so happened that I was in one of the two cribs against this back wall. Standing alone and looking at two cribs — one facing out and the other facing the wall, not knowing which baby was hers and fearing that somebody had put her baby up for adoption — my mother went insane. She began screaming and rushed to read the names on the two cribs.

A nurse burst in to calm my mom and asked her what she needed.

"I want to see my baby!" she kept screaming. "I want to see my baby!"

"Calm down, miss!"

"I will not calm down until I see my baby! You have all been lying to me about squeaky doors and perfect babies and I don't believe any of it!"

"OK, OK! Please relax. Here is your baby girl."

The nurse reached into the crib not facing the wall and, staring only at my mother, lifted me up. My mother gasped because I was totally covered in meconium. I guess I had not been checked on in a while and had managed to cover myself in the blackish green poop that comes out of newborns. This was, in fact, a sign that I was healthy, but the nurse almost dropped me the moment she saw that she was holding a slippery little, flailing dark-green monster.

"This is the squeaking door, Mrs. Shields. I'll clean her up and you can hold her." From that moment on, Mom never wanted to let me out of her sight again.

They released us from the hospital once I gained a bit of weight. Breast-feeding didn't seem to be popular in 1965, and I guess my mother never even considered it. I was put on Enfamil and sent home.

Evidently, Mom said that my eyes had remained closed since birth. She brought me home and waited but began to get worried because my eyes stayed shut. Well, Mom brought me back to the doctor, who said, "Oh, you want her eyes open?"

And with Mom's nod he took his big middle finger and thumb and flicked as hard as he could on the bottom of my feet. My eyes popped right open and I let out a wail and started to cry.

"There you go."

How rude! I had been born two months premature, so maybe I was just not ready to actually see the big world yet. You try getting out of a cozy bed two months before it's time to get up!

My father wanted to name me after his mother but Mom preferred the name Brooke. She had seen a beautiful photo of a woman in a field, and the photographer was named Christian Brooks. She thought

Brooke with an *e* instead of an *s* would be a pretty name for a girl. When the time came for me to be baptized, the priest said that because there was no saint named Brooke, I could not be christened Brooke. Mom says she immediately responded by saying: "Well, put an *a* at the end of Christ. Is that Catholic enough for ya?" I assume the name Christa also had something to do with the photographer, but her reported response to the priest made for a better tale.

So I was born Brooke Christa Shields and baptized Christa Brooke Shields. After the christening my mom and dad went to P. J. Clarke's and placed me on the bar and toasted me. My husband and I have done the very same thing with both our daughters. Celebrating with a beer to the baby on the bar has become a bit of a tradition. I have never been called Christa but always liked it as a middle name.

My mother was terrified of SIDS. A politician's child had recently died of crib death, and Mom could not get the thought out of her mind. She slept with me literally strapped to her chest and repeatedly held up a mirror to my mouth and nose to make sure I was breathing. The steam from my breath became her source of calm. I was a terrible eater and ate only half an ounce every half hour. Mom said she would pre-make countless bottles filled with half-ounce bottles of formula in a cooler next to her bed and feed me accordingly. This went on for some time, and after about six months, I was transferred to my wooden crib. I soon started pulling myself up in my crib and used the rails as a teething surface.

Mom and I became obviously physically bonded and my dad remained seemingly less knowledgeable and comfortable with his baby. One day Mom passed by the bathroom while my dad was in the shower. I was in need of my bath and Mom suggested to my dad he shower with me and get me cleaned up at the same time. He took me and a bit later Mom passed by the bathroom again only to see my dad standing in the shower holding my little naked body but now wearing his blue boxers. Another time Mom went to church and left me alone with my father. We were using cloth diapers in those days, and when Mom returned I was lying completely naked in bed, and a huge pile of diapers lay on the floor. When asked what had happened, Dad explained he knew not how to clean the mess and that he had used the diapers like tissues. Needless to say, that month's diaper supply had been depleted. Clearly my father was in over his head with regard to being a dad.

Dad found out soon enough, though, that the mother of his child could be quite a troublemaker. During one argument between my mom and dad it somehow happened that Mom's bra had gotten torn. For the first time ever, Mom had bought a sexy red-lace bra, which she was wearing at the time of the fight. In addition to the torn bra, a chair got broken. It was rare for my parents to fight in any sort of physical way, so this must have been a pretty big argument or Mom was the one to do all the damage. A broken chair and a ripped brassiere were hardly out of the realm of possibility for her to destroy. In any case, on this particular Saturday it all happened and my father stormed out of the apartment. Where he was going, she didn't know, which must have made her even angrier.

My mother was not satisfied. She wanted to have the final word. So she decided to tie the torn red-lace remnants of her bra onto the spindles of the destroyed chair and hand-deliver them to the Racquet and Tennis Club of Manhattan. Now, the Racquet and Tennis Club was one of the oldest all-male clubs in New York City. It is an incredibly old-school, traditional institution, complete with leather-lined libraries for cigar smoking and backgammon and huge oil paintings of elaborate foxhunt scenes or dead geese lined up under the watchful eye of a skilled pointer. Women were not allowed to be members and never set foot past the entrance.

Well, my mother marched right up to the club, walked through the doors, with the broken wooden chair strategically draped with red-lace undergarments boldly labeled "Mr. Frank Shields from Mrs. Frank Shields," and deposited it all right in the middle of the lobby.

I'm sure the staff had no idea of how to react. What was this? I guess they decided it was an art installation of some kind for one of their members. It was the sixties. Packages, evidently, were to be claimed during the workweek only, so, as my mother told the story, this symbol of public humiliation sat in the middle of the lobby for the world to see over the entire weekend. Dad's mortification would be witnessed by many an esteemed colleague. His shame had thus been initiated. It remained true that while Mom wanted to be accepted by high society, she equally loved challenging its social mores and sexist rules. My dad's version of the fur-coat story had arrived in full force;

this should have sent up the proper red flags.

Looking back, I imagine that this incident was just one of many outrageous antics. It was not, however, enough to break them up — yet. I speculate that there was a power to her that he somehow could not resist. I believe that it was not dissimilar to the type of power his own mother wielded. No doubt my mother was unlike anyone else in his life.

He had relief, though, because he often traveled for work. Dad left once more for Europe and began writing letters to Mom from abroad.

What transpired over the next few months is documented by letters sent to my mother in very small, neat handwriting, usually on hotel stationery. In the letters from Dad, he expresses his confusion and sadness about the fact that his father had not been to visit Mom and the baby. His family was not the kind to have many family get-togethers. In his writing, Dad seems hurt by the fact that his father was not reaching out to me and Mom more. My father also worried that Mom was not getting any help. He said many times that he was concerned that she wasn't getting out enough and that she should really ask for some help so as to spend time on herself.

He also promised to give my mom more money when he could get it, and a real wedding in a church one day. At times he wrote of wiring money and wishing he could be sending more but Italian banks and the like were less than helpful. I am struck by the tenderness that Dad had for "little Brookie" and how sad he seemed to be away. He seemed quite sincere about wanting things to work out.

In one of his more vulnerable correspondences, he comments on the joy he felt receiving a Valentine's Day card from my mom and me. He said it made his day and he was sorry to be missing being with his "girls" on what had always been my mom's favorite holiday. It is heartbreaking to hear his vulnerable tone in the correspondences only to discover that he was about to experience a devastating blow.

Imagine my own shock at reading Dad's next letter, postmarked February 16, 1966, which read:

Mumsy, after receiving such a wonderful Valentine's cable, to receive your cable of this morning was a real shock and suddenly I am unable to think clearly. I have a feeling of loss, a sense of nothingness, no aspirations, no idea of what to do, and as a whole a very sick feeling inside. Up until this morning I didn't consider the impact of the meaning of divorced, which I have brought on myself, my wife, and baby. I am trying to reason that the decree is merely a legal document and not an emotional state which cannot be reversed or resolved. I wanted to start clean but I didn't see the necessity legally of anything more than a separation. . . . I want to be happy with the two of you as a family and I am not going to change my thinking. I think of you as my wife this time away from New York, and I hope to God that I can redeem myself in your eyes so as to bring us back together. . . . I am trying to put out of my mind the trip to Mexico. I just don't know. . . .

He was clearly confused and did not know how to continue. He did love my mom and they did have a child together, so maybe he believed a separation would help. But he seemed to be fooling himself. My mom was not going to wait for what she was feeling would be the inevitable. She feared they would not last, and although convinced my father wanted to try to do the right thing, she thought he would not be happy in the long run.

I have no letters from Mom to my dad during this time, but I found some diaries in which Mom wrote about how ashamed my father was of her: "I am a burden to him financially and especially socially," one entry read. "He's ashamed to be with me in public for fear I may say something that might embarrass him." Another one read, "I am too opinionated and don't act right in public. I give a cheap appearance. 'Cheesy' was the word he used."

She told me Dad would get exasperated with her and her "deez, dems, and doz" way of speaking. She felt my father was ashamed to be with her. She writes that he wanted her to be a different person with a different background. I believe Mom was afraid he would eventually reject her, and she wanted to save herself the pain.

She knew deep down that my father loved us but wanted a different life. Maybe she really was doing this for him, to set him free. I can't say what is actually the truth or what my mom's real insecurities were, but for some reason, she made a preemptive decision. My mother probably heard my father use the word *separation* and just made a rash choice.

She flew to Mexico, where it used to be the very easiest place to obtain a divorce on your own. Mom left me with Lila and got the divorce by herself. By the time Dad returned from Europe, my mom had declared herself a single mother.

What is so shocking and sad is how stunned my dad appeared by Mom's pronouncement. I don't think he was quite ready to be free from my mom, but I wonder if he was secretly a bit relieved.

Mom's actions often had an impulsive and self-destructive quality. She saw herself alone, and although I believe she craved love and partnership, she feared she was not worthy and therefore often jumped ship before she could get too hurt.

Now, however, she had this little baby who couldn't leave. She had a baby daughter who was completely dependent on her.

My mother explained to my father that she wanted neither alimony nor any kind of child support other than an education for me. She said she could take care of the two of us somehow but insisted that he send me to school all the way through college.

I doubt Dad talked about marriage again but they definitely took time to fully disengage with one another. They seemed to find a way to still spend a lot of time together because of me. He helped out when he could and they celebrated some holidays together for a couple of years. In fact I have many photos of us all together while I was a toddler and a young kid. It was as if without the pressure of being married, my dad could relax and love us both. They lived separately but eased out of one another's lives. I have no idea if it was painful for my mom during this period but I am sure his getting married again would have stung when it happened.

My father kept true to his word and paid for my entire formal education and was present and beaming on every graduation day.

So, although the whirlwind of life and the emotions that accompanied the events of 1964 and 1965 were fraught, they did not seem void of love and some version of respect and understanding.

CHAPTER THREE:
SHE COULD MAKE IT RAIN

Having never really known my parents as a couple, I had no feeling of loss or guilt surrounding their divorce. I would grow up knowing, or at least trying to know, them each independently. From the day I was born, whether they were a couple or not, my mom always made sure that my dad saw me frequently.

It was clear that my mother wanted my father to have a relationship with me. Even if she herself could not be with him, she wanted me in his life. She would invent ways for him to be forced to see me. Sometimes, if Dad hadn't seen me in a while, Mom would dress me up in a fancy dress or romper, complete with bonnet or bow and Mary Janes, and take me to the building in which my father worked. She'd do this at the end of his workday. Mom would wait with me just around the corner but with a good view of the building's entrance.

She would watch for my dad to leave, and as he came out of the building, she'd push me out alone and say, "Go, go see Daddy!" She told me she'd duck out of sight and I'd toddle over to him. Slightly surprised and a bit nervous for my safety, he'd scoop me up in his arms and search for my mom. When she popped out into view, he'd use his naturally booming voice and exclaim, "Jesus Christ, Teri, what the hell are you doing?"

After the ambush, I'm not sure if we all spent some time together or they just chatted on the street for a bit. I'm sure my dad usually had some place to go, but Mom was satisfied just knowing she made him see his baby girl. There was never a doubt in my mind that he was my dad.

I even have pictures of both Mom and Dad strolling me down Fifth Avenue during the Easter parade. In the photos I'm about two or three, and we look like a perfectly intact, happy family. Mom is chic in her black-and-white plaid skirt and cropped jacket with a white pillbox hat. Dad looks dapper as always, in a suit and tie. I am in a navy wool double-breasted coat and a white hat. My white tights were a bit twisted or saggy and dirty at the knees, but my black patent-leather Mary Janes are shiny. Together, they were a stunning couple and

always turned people's heads. They didn't look divorced.

But even though the photos make us look as if we were just like any other family, the truth was very different. From the time my parents divorced, my life with my mother was very unique. Surprisingly, being a single mom in New York City proved to be more convenient for Mom than one would think. I did have occasional sitters, and my godmother often watched me, but for the most part, I was portable and a welcomed accessory to any of my mother's fashion-forward outfits. Sporadically, she brought me by bus out to visit her mom and siblings in Paterson and Newark but, for the most part, we remained in good old Manhattan. Mom took me to parties with her various fashion-industry friends. We went to dinner clubs and movies and even the theatre, and I would either play or sleep and was obviously happier being with her than with a sitter. I was simply most comfortable being physically around my mother.

Although my mother managed to stay in contact with many of the friends she made while with my father, she also maintained the friendships she had cultivated outside his Waspy circles. She made new friends as well, many who were in the fashion industry or entertainment of some kind. She befriended photographers and stylists, designers and artists. She was developing a very colorful group of talented people from diverse walks of life. In any given week we would be visiting a huge mansion out in the Hamptons as well as going to a downtown evening in a jazz club or performance-art space or photo exhibit. She frequented all walks of life, with me in her arms and then on her hip. It appeared Mom began forging her own path.

I was one of those babies you see out late

at night in restaurants and being passed around the table to be cooed at or brought into the bathroom to be changed on the sink. I slept soundly, lulled by the low din of voices and silverware clinking. Everybody made sure to write "Don't forget to bring the baby" on invites to dinner parties and cocktail gatherings. I had very little fear of new people, and although most bonded to my mom, I would gladly go smile at a stranger. Some things never change. . . .

Mom always dressed me like a little doll. I wore smocked dresses and pressed cotton bloomer outfits with matching bonnets. I was always spanking clean and all dolled up. Mom put extra effort into my looking a girl because I had no hair and people repeatedly asked, "Oh, what's his name?" Mom taped little homemade pink mini ribbon bows to my head to ensure people knew I was a girl. But that still didn't work much of the time. Once, in an elevator, a woman scoffed to my mother, "Why would you do that? Why would you put a pink bow on a little boy's head?"

Mom told stories about my babyhood just like she used to tell stories about her own life. Some were true, some a bit embellished. One example of this happened while we were living on Fifty-Second Street. Mom let me crawl on the sidewalk before I learned how to walk. Evidently, one day, on one of these jaunts, we passed Greta Garbo's apartment building. Garbo herself just happened to be out on a walk, and as the story goes, she stopped, looked at me and then to my mother, nodded her head, and continued on her way. Mom took this as a literal nod of approval from a legend and believed I had been blessed and sanctioned as one destined to make a mark in the world. I do believe Garbo was walking and perhaps noticed this little kid crawling on her knees on the pavement and made some gesture to me, but the real meaning of the nod is open to interpretation. For all we know, the regal Garbo could have been looking disdainfully at this careless mother who was allowing her baby to rub her soft knees on cement streets. Or maybe she was, in fact, envisioning the future?

Mom and I were rarely apart from each other, and I'd do anything to make her happy and get her attention. When I was around four, she took me to a piano bar and I asked if I could go to the bathroom alone. The bathroom was a small place and tucked into an alcove. When I did not return quickly, Mom started to rise to come search for me. As she stood she started to hear my

voice over the sound system. She looked at the piano and I was seated atop it, legs crossed and singing a cappella. I don't remember if the piano player accompanied me or not, but according to my mom, my voice was heard throughout the club. I knew "Embraceable You" and "My Funny Valentine" were my mother's two favorite songs. She would often sing them to me, so I knew the words to both. I was offered the mike, chose "Embraceable You," and serenaded her. This particular club would later become La Cage aux Folles. We'd someday be among their favorite patrons, but I never did sing on the piano again.

Even before I could talk (or sing), people often remarked to my mother about my looks being rather extraordinary. My mom would boast that when I was an infant, people often stopped us to comment on my "beauty." Of course Mom thought her child was the most beautiful child in the world, but doesn't every mother think that?

One day, while riding in a checker cab, Mom was given an idea that may or may not have occurred to her previously. It was about her baby's looks and the possibility of using them to make a living. The story she told was that one spring day in 1966 a typical New York cab driver was driving her and her ten-month-old baby girl uptown in his cab. The driver glanced in his rearview mirror a few times and then exclaimed in an old New York accent, "Ya know dat liddle kid a yers? She should model!"

Evidently he had a two-year-old niece who had become a model. "Now the kid makes more than I do by the hour. Figure dat."

Mom thanked the cabbie for the compliment and the suggestion, gave him a nice tip, and exited the cab. But the idea stayed with her, and as fate would have it, a few weeks later one of her photographer friends phoned in a panic. "We need a baby who can kiss!" He was shooting an Ivory soap ad and was seeing countless babies for the campaign. The client was not happy with the selection. Not one baby out of hundreds he saw was the one. They were either not similar enough to the model chosen as the mom, not cute enough in a unique way, couldn't kiss, or they were simply hysterical. The baby had to know how to kiss, but that was the *last* thing any of these kids wanted to do at this moment. It was mayhem. Kids were screaming and the client was on the verge of tears.

The photographer begged my mother to bring me down to his studio. I vaguely feel like I can remember being carried through the chaos and cries. It could be that I have been told the story so many times that I imagine I actually remember. But as the story goes, it was midafternoon and I had already had my afternoon nap, so I was in great spirits. Being, as usual, comfortable and acclimated around adults, I was all smiles, and kisses, and curiosity. I got the job on the spot and was shot for the ad, holding a bar of soap out to my "mother" — no kissing involved after all. During the shoot I reportedly sat on the floor of the freshly white-painted set and opened twenty-four cases of Ivory soap, each containing twelve bars each. The client was thrilled and everybody was happy.

The relieved photographer scooped me up in his arms and hugged my mom for saving the day. To the world, that photographer was the already famous Francesco Scavullo. But to me, he was just "Uncle Frankie."

My modeling career had begun.

So by the ripe old age of eleven months I already had a major national ad under my belt. Mom realized that she had an opportunity and should follow up. I was not with any agency, so we had no percentage to give away and the money from this first job went solely to my mother and me. Mom had periodically worked part-time at Brentano's bookstore, but the salary would not cover child care and living expenses. Though not required, Dad did help out with the rent, but the chance for additional revenue being generated by us was clearly appealing.

Mom found me a manager named Barbara Jarrett, although it appears as if I did not have another big modeling job for a while. By the time I was two or three, however, I began to get jobs for catalogues and I spent the next few years being managed by both Mom and Barbara. I find it interesting that both my mom and I began working at a very young age. Cleaning houses and modeling are very different, but a certain work ethic was instilled in us both early on. Mom was imaginative and gutsy as a child and now she was being forthright and creative as a mother. She was turning chance into an opportunity.

I still had hardly any hair, so for the first two years I modeled primarily as a boy. Once, right before leaving on a location shoot for a catalogue in Jamaica, Barbara took my mom aside and said: "For God sake, don't take her bathing suit off around anybody. They think she's a boy."

As child models, we got paid to do the activities that we might not have always been able to afford ourselves. The trips were always a blast. The moms and the kids would meet early in the A.M. on a street corner and all load into a huge camper. They had fun drinks and snacks, and the drive was crazy, with kids playing and singing songs. I loved being on locations or checking into various tropical resorts and chasing lizards and being in the sun. It was usually the same basic group of kids who eventually became close and even longtime friends. These were some of my earliest and fondest memories of being a model.

I thought my mom could do no wrong. I believed she could even change the weather.

One day, when I was about four, she bought me a red patent-leather raincoat and matching rain hat. It was a sunny day but I still wanted to wear my new coat and hat. Mom insisted that it was unlikely that the rain would fall and that I'd be hot and uncomfortable. The way my mom told the story, I walked out of the apartment, and turning to her over my shoulder, I declared, "Don't worry, Mama, you'll make it rain." And, as the story goes, as soon as we went outside, the skies opened and there was a torrential downpour.

Around the time I was nine years old, my mother and I moved into an apartment on Seventy-Third Street between First and Second Avenues. It was on the seventh floor of a white brick building called the Morad Diplomat. I was close to my dad, but it was my mother to whom I was incredibly bonded. She was my everything. When we moved in, we had very little furniture. Our first night was spent on a queen-size mattress on the floor, pushed up to the wall. We had sheets, one down pillow, and large multicolored neon crocheted blanket that my mom had taken from a visit to her mother's apartment in Newark.

Mom slept with her back to the wall, and I was the inner spoon. I will always remember that I fell asleep peacefully and comfortably. It was one of the best night's sleep I can ever remember. To me, being spooned has always been an instant sleeping pill. This closeness with my mom gave me the utmost feeling of comfort and safety. In a way it was like being tied to her chest once again, only this time we were side by side. I think we both believed that we would forever exist within this dynamic. I loved the bed being up against the wall and spooning with Mom and being able to see the door. I was in a warm cocoon and had not a worry in the world. We were conjoined and content.

On those first nights I would say, "Hug me!" and my mom would wrap me up and drape her left arm over my side. She would always ask if her arm was too heavy. It never was, but even if it had been, I was too afraid she'd remove it if I said so. Instead, I always said it was fine. I'm not sure Mom ever gave me her full weight until she knew I was asleep.

I was becoming so enmeshed with my mother that it was as if my taste buds were affected. I liked Yodels until the day my mother tasted one and said it tasted "waxy."

After my next bite, I concurred and never ate another Yodel again. Actually, I'm not even sure if she disliked Yodels at all. She may have just wanted to get me to stop eating junk. But in any case, her opinions were strong enough to influence how I actually tasted my food.

I know she was drinking even then, but the effects weren't clear to me at such a young age. If anything, it seemed to make her more fun and more creative. My mother was always such a great artist and creative crafter. Each Halloween she made elaborate costumes for me. Starting from about three years old and for many years after, she did get off easy because I always went as Charlie Chaplin. I often won first prize for that costume and for my ability to imitate his recognizable waddle and circular cane swing. But as I grew up I began wanting to wear more fun or feminine costumes. One year she crafted me into a huge blooming red rose. My head popped out from the middle of a layered red crepe rose. She dressed my body in a green leotard and tights for the stem, and on each hand she gave me cuffs of green crepe-paper leaves. I wore the tights over my penny loafers and by the end of the night had worn through them by walking around. Another year

Mom made me an exact replica of a tube of Crest toothpaste. She perfectly copied the tube onto cardboard and even included the cap. I was transformed into a dental delight. I was thrilled with the precision of her rendering but it was extremely hard to walk in. I had to take geishalike steps and the edge of the cardboard cut into the front of my ankles. The pain didn't bother me, though, because it was such a creative costume, and I was proud my mom made it by herself.

Mom put so much time into my costumes I began to expect to win the contest at the gymnastics space, Sokol Hall, where we'd attend their annual party. Because we lived in an apartment building, trick-or-treating was easy and I could go alone with a friend. I'd invite a school buddy and we'd begin on the penthouse floor and work our way down. It took hours, and our pumpkin-head buckets would be overflowing by the time we got to the lobby apartments. This was the height of the razor-blade-in-the-apple panic, and I was never allowed to eat any of my loot until after Mom had done a thorough check. It was always fine because we knew every inhabitant in the building. I never actually ate all the candy I got. It usu-

ally got stale before I finished even half the bucket.

Another story I love was about my doll, Blabby. Blabby was a doll similar to the amazing Baby Tender Love dolls of the seventies that I adored, but she was more unique. She used to make a sound like a baby cooing when you squeezed her rubber stomach. I took her into the bath with me so many times, however, that the coo soon turned into a bark. Later, with my kid scissors, I cut off almost all her hair. She looked

rather punk and ahead of her time, but soon, because of the baths and the brushing, it all fell out.

Blabby went everywhere with me. When we traveled by plane, Mom would strap her in with me in the seat. The seat belt went around us both and was fastened only when Blabby gave a "nod" that it was tight.

When I was around six years old, Mom and I had a layover in some city on our way back to New York. I had left Blabby in the terminal while waiting for our connection and playing some Pac-Man–type game. We hadn't noticed until Mom was strapping me into my seat and realized Blabby wasn't on my lap. The plane had begun its taxi on the runway when my mother suddenly and frantically called for the flight attendant. She told me not to say a word and then looked straight into the stewardess's eyes and calmly and emotionally, but deadly seriously, said, "We must get off this plane! It is a matter of life and death."

This was way before 9/11, and security was much more lenient. The flight attendant must have been alarmed enough, though, so she went to the cockpit and they stopped the taxi and returned to the gate to let both of us off. Mom and I deplaned without saying another word and I went directly to the game I had played before boarding the plane. Blabby was not there, so we tried lost and found. We reported Blabby's physical profile and had been waiting for over an hour when, from a distance, we saw a male airline official walking toward us, holding something behind his back. He was hiding my doll with an air of embarrassment and was, no doubt, relieved to returned her to me. Well, he could not have been more relieved than I was. I knew my mom would fix the situation.

I still have Blabby. But because she is bald and now has a large split down the middle of her head, my girls say she is "creepy." I don't agree. I have never before, nor since, seen a doll similar to her. Mom had given her to me, and after she died I put her necklace on Blabby. Creepy or not, she still sits in my room and reminds me of the time my mother stopped a 747 on a runway to retrieve my baby doll.

Mom probably loved the fact that she could wield that type of power. She always said that as long as you remain firm in your opinions and in their delivery — even if you're not telling the entire truth or you're not completely clear — you'd be surprised at what you can achieve.

Mom has been an unconventional person her whole life, and she wasn't about to change just because she had become a mother. She continued to take me to bars even as I got older. I remember when she taught me to shoot pool from behind my back. I couldn't have been older than eight and I learned fast. When I'd excitedly called my father and said, "Dad! I just learned how to shoot pool from behind my back," I remember him saying: "Where are you?"

"At a bar," I said.

"Jesus Christ."

I'm sure Dad wasn't thrilled with any of

this, but I was seemingly safe and having fun, and my mother seemed in control. The argument was tough to have.

The most useful bar talent I acquired — before learning how to tie a knot in a cherry stem with my tongue — involved holding up twelve sugar cubes stacked in between my thumb and pinky finger. It was this skill that I would use as the beginning of a conversation with the one and only Jackie Onassis.

Mom and I were at her long-standing favorite bar, P. J. Clarke's, when Mom spotted Jackie and Aristotle sitting at the tiny window seat in the empty middle section of the restaurant. It was their table! Mom said, "Brookie, that's the mother of the boy you are going to grow up and marry." Without waiting for permission, I leapt up and went over to the table to politely introduce myself.

I evidently went right up, said, "Hi, when I grow up, I am going to marry your son." Jackie said, "Oooh . . . ," as if the thought of her little boy growing up was too much to think of. I then showed her how to hold as many sugar cubes as she could between her two fingers. I simply showed her how to do this trick and then returned to my table. My mom claimed she was embarrassed, but it made for a great story and she loved to tell it.

Mom's version of discipline was unconventional. She was creative with punishments. I once begged her to let me have Devil Dogs for dinner. I cried, pleaded, and threw a tantrum, wanting this cakey, creamy, artificially made dessert snack for my meal. Mom finally conceded but said that if I really wanted Devil Dogs for dinner, I'd have to eat twelve of them. I thought I had hit the junk food jackpot until the third one brushed the roof of my mouth. I started to feel sick and ended up throwing up all over the bathroom. Mom simply asked if I ever wanted Devil Dogs for dinner again. I don't believe I have ever had one since. (Two major cakey junk foods crossed off my list!)

She wasn't afraid to embarrass herself, if necessary, to make a point. She once took my cousin Johnny to see *Godzilla* (which he called *Godzillabones*) and he threw a tantrum when leaving the theater. She immediately got down on the floor and threw her own tantrum, shocking Johnny and showing, once again, how creative — and effective — her discipline could be.

Some of the stories Mom thought were funny could also be scary. She was great at imitations, and most of them I loved because they made me laugh. But the one I did not enjoy at all was her imitation of the Witch in *Snow White.* In the animated movie the witch had this horrible and terrifying cackle that my mom could copy flawlessly. She would do it randomly and it unsettled me horribly. I'd beg her to stop; she'd continue the imitation for longer than I would have liked. I loved her ability to mimic and I consider my talent in this area a gift from her, but the minute Mom started with the voice, I'd start chanting, "You're my mother, you're my mother!" She simply wanted to do what she wanted to do and loved the attention. I don't think Mom ever knew I was actually, honestly scared. She would later tell this story and beam with pride at the fact that I kept repeating that she was my mother.

During these years my modeling career really began to take off. Mom was my manager, but she was hardly the typical "stage mother" one would have expected. She'd ask if I wanted to go in for a job and then simply let me do my thing. She never grilled me on how it went inside the rooms and instead waited for me to volunteer information. I am sure she would have loved getting feedback, but I don't remember her ever pressing me. When I did not get the job, she would just brush it off and we'd discuss what we should do with that free time. There were many times we'd hear parents through the elevator door screaming at their kids or even slapping them. We often heard the sound of crying getting fainter as the elevator descended to the first floor. I never understood why moms promised their kids things like bicycles if the kids agreed to go in on a "go see."

If the kid didn't want to model, I thought he shouldn't have to. My mother never bribed me or forced me to audition or work on things or on days I didn't feel like it. Granted, I was quite young and hardly ever stood up to my mom, but I don't recollect feeling pressured, like I was being forced to do something I didn't want to do. Mom made me feel that it was all my choice. She'd say I could stop anytime I wanted to. I, of course, wanted nothing more than to please her, so I rarely refused to do anything. On any particular day, if I ever expressed not wanting to go in for a job, Mom would unplug the phone or we would escape the house and go to Central Park.

This infuriated clients and agencies, but it ironically made me more sought after. *No* is a powerful word.

Strangely enough, I got only a few jobs in commercials. I was cast in a Johnson and Johnson Band-Aid ad and a Holly Hobbie doll commercial, but it quickly seemed that my looks were not considered all-American enough, and I was often turned down and labeled "too European." Whenever I did get a job, I knew I'd have fun no matter what, and my mom would feel happy. It was a win-win situation.

I learned early on that the sweeter I was to the adults, the nicer they treated me. It was all just for fun during those years, or at least it seemed that way to me.

I stayed at my grade school in Manhattan while working and rarely missed a day to model. On some of the bigger trips, I might miss a Friday. Even as I got older, Mom maintained this rule. If the agency phoned to say I had a shoot for 10:00 A.M. on a Thursday, Mom would respond by saying that was great and we would see them all at 3:00. If they pushed, she'd claim that if they didn't want me, it was fine to choose another child, but I would not be available until after school let out at 2:40. Basically, while other kids were involved in after-school sports or playdates, I was shooting for various catalogues. I can't say I minded not playing sports or being forced to spend any time separated from my mother.

I have a lot of great memories from these early years. I was once cast as Jean Shrimpton's daughter in an ad. Mom always said that I looked more like her than any other model or actress. Mom thought she was beautiful and had a face with perfect symmetry.

Over the next few years I modeled in ads and catalogues for Macy's, Sears and Roebuck, Bloomingdale's, Alexander's, McCall's, and Butterick. Whenever I had a "go see," Mom remained in the background. On set, Mom was not one of the moms who made her presence imposing. She never hovered over the creative team or offered unsolicited direction to me. She saw everything and had her opinions about everybody, but during these days, she was more subtle and did not share her judgments with me.

Our life was active and fun. We basically each had a full-blown career. I modeled and Mom managed.

By the time I was ten, it became obvious that I was in need of larger and more credible representation. Mom looked around at the various available children's agencies for models and was evidently dissatisfied with what she found. Even then, she had high aspirations and was not content settling for anything she deemed commonplace or plebeian.

Because she frequented many photographers' studios and artists' lofts socially and had friends who worked at cosmetic and hair care–oriented companies, she knew the best in the business. The models she loved all seemed to be represented by the Ford Modeling Agency and she knew the top ad agencies looked to them for their talent. Ford was an agency with such prestige and power that Mom decided it was the only suitable place for her baby girl.

In 1974, Ford Models did not have a children's department and had no plans of incorporating one into their already thriving business. But we had an in. Eileen and Jerry Ford, who had started Ford Models, knew my father from various social circles and from supplying models for Revlon ads, and my dad was now working for Revlon as a sales executive.

I remember that my mother had met Eileen and Jerry many times. They had all remained friendly, so Mom decided to approach Eileen personally. She loved to tell the story about how one day she opened the door and marched up the three flights to Eileen Ford's spacious and bright office.

Mom said she stood in front of Eileen's desk with her hands on her hips and explained to Eileen, "This agency doesn't have a children's division, and it should. Brooke will be your first child model."

Eileen was initially against it because she did not want to represent children. She turned my mom down. I am sure my mother did not appreciate being told no and would never admit it happened that way. Mom instead intimated that it was on that fateful day that she changed my future and helped make Ford a success. Ford did eventually begin a children's division that remains today. I was *not* the first child model to join, as I had been led to believe. Mom always claimed credit for being the woman who convinced Eileen Ford to start the Ford children's division. But did she at least plant the seed?

Somehow, as time went on, I began thinking there was something wrong with my mom's drinking. We were so busy that it was easy to overlook, but looking back, I see that although I would not have had the vocabulary to articulate it at the time, I realized that Mom was a highly functioning alcoholic.

She kept it hidden for years, but the signs

were there, even if I was too young to see them. I recently met a man at a funeral who said that when I was two or three he lived in an apartment on East Seventy-Ninth Street and Mom lived temporarily on a floor above him. He had met her with my father and they had become friends. He told me that Mom would sometimes knock on his door in the evenings and say, "I'm going out for a drink. Here, just take her for a bit."

She would leave me there and we would hang out. It would be 10:00 or 11:00 P.M. He and I would just climb into bed and fall asleep. He said he never knew what time it would be, but Mom would eventually return and take me back upstairs. It is a bit sad to think that Mom just dropped me off so she could go drink, but at least she wasn't keeping me out all night.

Still, Mom was the world to me, both at home and when I was working, and we had wonderful times together, but they were increasingly tempered by alcohol. She managed to keep our lives going for years before it would become a more obvious and debilitating problem; the negative effects becoming undeniable. In addition, it's equally surprising to see how humorous the results of her drinking actually were early on.

Mom went to church every Sunday, no matter where she was. I was raised Catholic and completed catechism to receive my first Holy Communion and was also later confirmed. Every Sunday I accompanied her to this little church on Seventy-First Street and Second Avenue. It was there that I sang my first song on stage, for the Saint Patrick's Day concert. I sang "When Irish Eyes Are Smiling" and was so nervous I twisted the bottom of my green velvet dress into such a balled-up knot that I showed my white big-girl pants to the entire congregation. I won first prize but will never be sure if it was for the song or my early attempts at striptease.

Mom and I were once at Mass and I was not aware that she was hungover. I was still rather naïve about such a thing as a hangover and she must have done a lot of her drinking alone or while I slept. Mom dozed off during the sermon and I did not even realize it until the moment when the congregation stood up. We all stood up, as did my mom, except she began to start vigorously clapping. She must have thought she was at the theatre and tried to cover it up by pretending she was brushing dust or lint off various articles of her clothing. It was a scene worthy of a Lucille Ball sketch and we would retell it for decades. It just seemed funny then.

But at some point, her drinking stopped being funny. One day when I was in third grade my mom and I were walking to school and chatting. I remember thinking that I wished I knew my mother only in the mornings. She was never drunk before school. She may have been hungover but I never knew it. I realized she never drank before school, but, come 3:00, I knew I'd find her in an altered state. It became inevitable that when school was out and she came to pick me up, she'd have the look in her now slightly glassy eyes. I needed only to see the dryness of her lips to know she had been drinking.

Once at night, soon after detecting her pattern, I blurted out how I felt. I don't remember her response, but even when I declared in anger how I wished I knew her only in the mornings, her behavior had not altered. I can't imagine having an addiction so powerful that a comment like this from a child would leave me unchanged.

If Mom wasn't at home for some reason and I had been at a friend's apartment, I knew where to find her. There was a bar at Seventy-Third and First Avenue on the northwest side of the street called Finnegans Wake. I could either locate her there or farther down Third Avenue at an Italian restaurant called Piccolo Mondo. It was always such a physical relief to see her that I began overlooking the fact that she was on her way to being drunk, if not already there. Usually either I convinced her to come home or we sometimes had some food and then returned home to watch some TV. Mom was rarely violent, and it would probably have been easier for me to admit to her disease if I was ever physically abused.

My particular abuse was much more subtle and created a longer-lasting impact. Because every time Mom drank, she left me. I was not able to articulate this until years later and only after a great deal of soul-searching and therapy. I felt abandoned by her when she drank, but as long as I wasn't hurt and she was accounted for and alive, I could justify that everything was all right. Never really knowing what I was going to come home to established a constant underlying sense of anxiety in my gut. I remained unrealistically optimistic that every day would be different. Mom would keep her promise and not get drunk at that birthday or that particular function.

More and more, I began to understand the blueprint of my mother's drinking on a deeper level. I remember not knowing how

Dear Mom,

I just want to say thank you for being so very good about drinking. I love you for that (not only that) I also feel that we are happier together when you are not drinking. We dont fight as much, we laugh more and have much more fun, I love it, I really do. I wish you could see yourself and me when you are in that state, it is real hateful.

Mommy I beg of you please stay without drinki and also PLEASE can we not got to the rice and beans place tonight, it takes so long and I love it when you eat at home, I admit I don help at all with dinner bu I promise from now on I will set and clear th

104

to complain to her about it. I always felt taken care of and deeply loved and she had not yet become as verbally abusive as she would in years to come. I tried to find ways to show her that her drinking was becoming an issue. It started off subtly: I would suggest Mom just drink ginger ale with me at dinner, for example, or I'd say, "Hey, Mama, maybe you don't have to drink tonight. And we can watch a movie." She assured me it was all fine and then simply did as she pleased. Sometimes she was smart enough to curb it for a while, and then when I had seemingly relaxed a bit, she'd resume more heavily.

Mom was never one to enjoy decorating the Christmas tree. One particular Christmas Eve, after going to midnight Mass and a local diner that served alcohol, we came home. I needed to finish decorating, and while I was focused on the tree, Mom must have fallen asleep. When I turned to ask her what she thought, she responded only by snoring. She basically passed out on the couch, and at that moment I immediately saw a way to show her she had a problem. I chose not to awaken her. It was a risk I had to take. It all had to do with trying to catch her in some way, so that I could legitimately blame her drinking for my unhappiness. In earlier years I would have just awakened her and pretended, both that the guy with the red suit was real and that her drinking was not a problem.

If Mom woke up on her own and dealt with Christmas presents under the tree, then it was proof, I told myself, that Santa existed and her alcohol consumption was, in fact, not that bad. If she stayed asleep and could not rally to play Santa, I could accuse her of passing out and ruining Christmas. I could say, "See, there is *no* Santa and because you were drunk, I now know and I am crushed. I hate you and I hate your drinking." This was the year reality hit me, and the blow was threefold. Mom was a drunk, there was no Santa, and Mom's drinking ruined Christmas. And, in a way, everything.

CHAPTER FOUR:
IF YOU DIE, I DIE

Throughout both the closeness and turmoil of living with my mother, I always had something else, which was my relationship with my father and his family. I spent quite a lot of time with him in the Hamptons, where my Pop-Pop, the former tennis champion, was something of a legend at the Meadow Club of Southampton. Mom and I would spend the summers out there, visiting with my dad and enjoying the beach club where my father was a member. We didn't have a house of our own, but Mom wanted me to know my dad and be a part of the privileged existence that was available via his upbringing.

We at first stayed at friends' houses or with relatives of my father's, but we also rented a room above Herrick Hardware in the town of Southampton. I attended day camp and spent my days at the beach club, where I learned how to swim in the large, rectangular, seemingly Olympic-size pool. There are many pictures of me and my little friends eating hot dogs or ice cream, wearing our little Lilly Pulitzer floral bathing-suit bottoms and no tops.

When I was a baby, Mom took me to the Meadow Club when invited, and as I got older she would drop me off at the club mid-morning and I'd be watched by various mothers and families who welcomed me as their own. I am not sure what my mom did during the times I was at the beach club, but I don't remember her being with me there all the time. She would have had to have been specifically invited, because she was not a member. Mom managed to stay busy. She befriended a bartender at a place called Shippy's. It was in town and a popular joint for food and drink. It basically became Mom's go-to watering hole. She had her haunts in every town we inhabited. I imagine Mom spent many hours at that particular establishment sidled up to the dark wood bar.

There is something tragic in the thought of my being introduced to and accepted by a part of society in which my own mother existed solely on the periphery. She never let on if she felt like an outsider or if she coveted a closer membership to this more

rarified world. Looking back, it seems that once again she enjoyed straddling the fence that separated the Waspy culture from her Newark roots. She enjoyed knowing the locals as well as the wealthier set.

At the end of the beach day, when all the other kids returned to their big houses by the sea, I was either picked up or returned to the small rented walk-up room over Herrick's. It was a very modest space. The tub stood in the kitchen and was covered by a long wooden lid. In order to bathe, one would lift the wooden countertop and fill the tub. My father stayed with various friends and relatives who had stunning properties a short distance from the ocean with rolling lawns, pools, and guesthouses. I was happy anywhere and bounced between the mansions and our single room. I have to believe I welcomed the proximity of my mom in this tiny space. I felt uneasy, sometimes, in the vastness of these other homes and felt safe in our insulated shell. I was also still so young that I didn't recognize the disparity in socioeconomic status evident in the varied living arrangements.

One night when I was a bit older, maybe five or six, Mom and I were with my friend Lyda at a dinner party at a friend's house way out in the potato fields. My mother and Lyda's mother had been pregnant at the same time and were both single mothers. They had a special bond, and in turn, "Lydes" and I became the closest of friends. Her grandmother had a house out in Southampton and much of our summer was spent with them.

On this particular night Mom had been drinking pretty heavily throughout the evening. The adults were all sitting around in the living room after dinner, and the kids were playing on the floor. Mom commented on one little girl's beautiful head of hair. She then reached out to touch it and, in doing so, lost her balance. Mom always wore many rings, sometimes on all her fingers except the thumb. One of Mom's rings got caught in the little girl's hair and she got yanked down with Mom's hand. The girl's mother got very angry and accused my mom of purposely pulling her child's hair. She said she wanted her to stay away from her daughter.

Mom, uncharacteristically, did not put up a fight. The plan had been for all of us to spend the night, but the ring incident shook us all up. Lyda called her grandmother, who soon arrived. Lyda said to me, "You know, Brookie, you can come to my grandmother's if you want."

I explained that I had to stay with my mom. I needed to make sure she was OK.

Even then, I realized something wasn't quite right. "You're so lucky, Lyda, that you have someplace to go," I added.

I was a young child, but I was more worried for my mom's safety than for my own. Sure, I would have preferred the warmth and comfort and safety of the cozy and beautifully decorated guest room in a drama-free home, but I had a deeply embedded sense of loyalty and obligation to my mom and her well-being. I could never abandon my mother by choosing to stay with my friend over her. I was the only one around to take care of my mom and I was constantly worried that something would happen to her. I had made an unspoken promise to continue to be by her side and protect her from harm, and I wasn't going to let this episode change that.

I am pretty sure we never socialized with that particular family again, and I imagine that this incident fueled gossip about my mother's drinking and her conduct. I never understood why Mom did not convince others of her innocence. It had begun as a warm gesture toward this little blond girl. Also, why would a grown woman purposely yank a little kid's hair? It all seemed kind of unfair to me, and I felt embarrassed and sad for my mom.

Over the years, I also had fun memories of both the beach club and hanging with the year-round local community. I remember being welcomed by the polarized world and not really even noticing the differences.

For many years, I was too young to understand social barriers. I had been taught very strict manners by my mother. Other mothers would comment on how polite and well-behaved I was, and I was always invited for playdates. On one particular playdate I brought my plate to the kitchen sink at the conclusion of the meal. I was quickly reprimanded by the mother and informed that I needn't do such a thing.

"But my mommy said I should always bring my plate to the sink."

When I returned home, my mother got a phone call from this particular woman, who said, "Please tell your daughter that we have people working for us who clear the table. When she visits, she does not have to bring her plate to the kitchen sink."

"Well, we *don't* have people who do that for us, and you need not worry about her doing it again in your home, because my daughter will not be returning there again for a playdate. Good-bye."

Mom laughed when she told the story later, loving that a woman from Newark had taught her daughter better manners than people who had more money than we would ever have.

When I was five years old, Dad married Didi Auchincloss. It was on May 1, 1970, in Manhattan. Didi was from a prominent New York family and had been traditionally educated. She had been married previously but was divorced from Tom Auchincloss, who was Jackie Kennedy's stepbrother.

I don't remember them meeting or dating, just that one day I was told Dad was getting married. Because I had never experienced my mother and father as a married couple living together and as a bonded couple, I felt no jealousy toward my dad's new bride. In fact, I thought she was very pretty and that everything in her house was always so neat. She was petite and reserved and kept her life in strict order. She was a brunette, well-bred, and well-educated debutante who reminded me of Jackie Onassis. Dad had chosen the antithesis of my mother. This, without a doubt, must have killed Mom. There is a beautiful photo of a smiling Dad and Didi coming out of an Upper East Side church and crossing the street. Dad is in tails and Didi has flowers in her hair. To me, it all seemed beautiful and perfect. I used to stare at every detail of this photo when I visited their Eighty-Sixth Street apartment. It all just looked so classic and beautiful.

Didi had two children from her first marriage. Her daughter, Diana, was six years old, and her son, Tommy, was nine. I suddenly had an instant family, and I was excited by the future. It wasn't long before another baby was on the horizon. My

stepsister, Diana, and I were very lucky that our parents married, and even though we did not know it at the time, we were to become partners, allies, confidants, and lifelong sisters.

Didi gave birth to my first half sister, Marina, when Diana and I were seven and six, respectively. Imagine the joy of knowing I was an older sister and that there was now a baby to play with! I had wished that my mom would have another baby, but it was not possible. I vaguely remember her going into a hospital and having a "female operation." I suggested we adopt: "Just get one from the foundling home." I didn't want her with a man, but I did want a baby sibling. Now I had one, and Mom was off the hook.

Over the years, Diana and I began spending more and more time together and unabashedly laughing the whole time. Diana even became quite attached to my mother, and Mom often introduced us as her daughters. Talk about unconventional! Didi seemed to have no qualms about her firstborn daughter being in the company of her husband's ex-wife. She allowed Diana to spend time — a great deal of time — in our company and in our small-by-comparison apartment on Seventy-Third Street. Later, she even traveled with my mom and me all over the world. Diana and I became extremely close, and my mom loved us both. All parties involved seemed to support our being together. The three of us became a real team and we all benefited. Diana confided in my mother, who authentically loved her. I now had a partner with whom to commiserate. During the times Diana stayed with my mother and me, it seemed like we were always having fun and laughing.

Soon Dad and Didi moved out to the North Shore of Long Island. They bought a beautiful house in an area called Meadowspring. The house was huge and the backyard ample. I shared a room with Diana during my visits, and Tom and Marina had their own rooms.

Over the next seven years, little girls would be born into this growing brood. Cristiana next and Olympia "the baby."

Sometimes Diana would stay in the city with my mom and me. The three of us would drive around in our silver convertible, with the top down, eating cherries or peaches from the fruit stand. We would park outside Dad's office with the radio blaring, eating our fruit and awaiting my father, who would drive Diana back out to Long Island. It was slightly reminiscent of when Mom used to wait to surprise-attack my father outside his old office building. This time it was slightly more intended to create a stir. Picture an old silver convertible, its top down, loud music and laughter blaring from it, parked in front of a Park Avenue office building filled with investment bankers and CEOs.

Sometimes Dad picked us both up and

sometimes just Diana. I spent many week-ends out on Long Island with Dad's family and accompanied them on spring breaks in the Bahamas. I had two totally different lives and seemed to go in and out of each with ease. At my dad's there was routine and a schedule we strictly adhered to. There were three meals each day, served at roughly the same times. Kids washed up for meals and often ate with the nanny. During dinner parties, the adults ate in the dining room while the kids stayed in the big kitchen. On days that Dad came back late from work in Manhattan, Didi or the nanny would create a plate for him that he just had to heat up. There was very little in terms of surprise. At the end of the day you could always find my dad sitting in his study watching the boob tube. Bedtimes were set in stone, and only late-night whispering delayed actual sleep.

By stark contrast, Mom had no set meal-times. We often ate out at various Chinese or Italian restaurants later than conventional mealtimes for children. We rarely cooked breakfast but instead went to the corner deli for a buttered roll with coffee and copies of the *Daily News* and the *Post*. We'd read each other our horoscopes and enjoyed the taste of the sweet butter on a hard roll. There was always the perfect amount of crunch on the outside and soft on the inside. My coffee was mostly milk and sugar but I loved being able to order "The regular, please."

That was our routine and we craved it. With Mom I never had a nanny and only rarely a sitter. Mom and I went to see movies and off-Broadway shows. We'd stay up late and didn't always get up on time for school.

But by the time visits to my dad's rolled around, I welcomed the change of pace. I loved having the option of varied and contrasting lifestyles. The structure that my dad's world provided was a tremendous relief from the adventurous and more Bohemian existence I lived with my mother. In the same way, the lack of routine and spontaneity with Mom served as a welcome reprieve after living under my stepmother's roof.

This duality, however, would create confusion later. Not clearly adopting any one side would later prove to be perplexing. Where did I really belong? It was as if I were living two parallel lives. The environment my father provided was the antithesis of that in which I lived with my single mom.

However, I was so enmeshed with my own mother that even though I looked forward to the order I felt in my father's house and knew how included I was as a family member, I was not open to my stepmother as a symbol of anything maternal. I once put ice down our English nanny's shirt and ran from her only to fall and split open my knee. I was rushed to the hospital and definitely needed stitches. Didi came in with me as I lay down on the bed to be sewn up for the first time in my life. She warmly tried to hold my hand while the doctor stitched me up, but I refused. Gripping the side of the bed with one hand and holding a clump of the hair on the back of my head with the other, I defiantly stated, "No, thank you. You are not my mother."

I did not dislike my stepmother — not in the least — or that my dad had a new wife. But I was simply not attached. I made it clear that nobody in the universe could fill my mother's shoes. And with all due respect, Didi never tried. My stepmom was the antithesis of my mother. She was tiny, systematic, and never prone to drama. She believed in protocol and lists. She was fastidious and was even known to alphabetize her spices. I used to do anything I could to unsettle her. I loved screaming and having her run into the kitchen, worried I had been hurt again, only to greet her with

"Ahhh! Does the cayenne pepper go with *C* or *P*?"

She always smelled good and maintained her own nails. I'd often smell the enamel from down the hall and knew the color she picked would be a subtle one. I made sure to paint my nails black whenever I visited. Didi always wore an array of yellow-gold bangles and bracelets. To this day, if I hear a jingling of bracelets, she comes to mind.

By contrast, my mom was larger than life, disorganized, and often incited chaos. She was frequently boisterous, she drank and cursed like a construction worker, and she wore red lipstick and fire engine–red nail polish. She was clean but often disheveled. Mom's idea of order was writing important phone numbers on tiny scraps of paper and losing them and tying up her credit cards with one of the thousands of rubber bands she had saved from delivered newspapers.

My mother never seemed outwardly resentful about the other life that I had at my father's, but there were signs that she wasn't fully accepting of all it represented. She tried to control it. For instance, at the beginning of every summer, Dad took me to get my annual pair of Top-Siders and a few Lacoste short-sleeve shirts. I loved these outings and couldn't wait to wear what I knew the other kids would be wearing. Mom shopped for me only at thrift stores and would never buy me brand labels. In fact, every time I came home with a Lacoste shirt, Mom would painstakingly cut out the little signature alligator. This was not an easy task because the thread was a sturdy plastic, and a hole would inevitably be left. Mom would then sew up the hole with the same color of thread as the shirt, and even though they were brand-new, they looked secondhand. Only then was I allowed to wear the now no-name item. It amazes me how much she coveted the world of privilege yet thwarted its symbols. It was a confusing time for me, but I knew I was loved by both sides. They were each protecting me and caring for me in their individual ways and from their unique perspectives.

Overall, there was a good relationship between the two families. I have always been pleasantly surprised and deeply relieved that neither my mother, nor my father, nor my stepmother ever spoke ill of one another. Nor did they try to pit me against the other family or try to prove their superiority. I went back and forth frequently and never felt like a traitor.

One thing that never changed was my devotion to my mother and the feeling that our lives would be forever intertwined. The brakes on our new black Jeep once went out while we were traveling across the George Washington Bridge heading out to New Jersey.

Mom screamed for me to get in the backseat and strap in because we had no way of stopping. I refused. I remember feeling strangely proud and looking straight ahead and saying, "No! If you die, I die." I was steadfast.

We veered off the bridge, onto the Palisades Parkway, and up an incline, eventually slowing to safety. We shut off the engine and were fine, but that Jeep model and year was soon after recalled. I am sure I remember the event so vividly because Mom herself loved telling the story of how her daughter would rather die than be without her. She got to hear me pledge my undaunted love for her. What more could she ever want?

I continued modeling throughout my childhood. I was getting a few more commercials and did one for Tuesday Taylor, a Barbie-like doll whose ponytail grew when you pushed a button. This one was fun because I got to keep one of the dolls while the other girl got to take home Piper, her sister. I also did a Susie Q's spot, which was not nearly as fun because I had to eat Susie Q's all day and got supersick. It was a commercial with Mason Reese, and I remember thinking his mom was a real character.

When I was nine years old, I was cast in my first film, then titled *Communion,* which was later changed to *Alice, Sweet Alice.* The film was a horror story in which my character gets tortured by her older sister and is eventually murdered. It mostly takes place inside a church and during the young sister's first Holy Communion. The casting process was an odd one, and the story of my audition became an anecdote my mother loved to repeat to anybody who'd listen. As usual, I went into the room by myself while Mom waited outside. I was then asked how I would pretend I was being strangled. Funnily enough, I was at the age when my friends and I did this crazy thing with our breath that always made me laugh. We'd push all the air out of our mouths and then do this deep, guttural, crazy machine-gun laugh until our faces got completely red and puffy and we became hysterical. Because our faces were so red and our eyes filled with tears, it looked kind of disgusting and scary. So I was very ready to pretend to be strangled.

I was told that in the pivotal death scene, my character was to get strangled with a candle, stuffed in a deacon's bench, and set on fire. A deacon's bench most commonly found in churches and chapels is where the deacon or priest sits during the Mass. It's usually wooden, with a spindled back and arms. During the audition, in a room full of people, I proceeded to do the demonstration of my suffocating red face. I held my breath, bore down, and let out a huge fart. I was incredibly embarrassed and quickly mentioned that during the actual filming I would not do that.

Later that same day, after having gotten the part, I showed up for rehearsal. A group of actors were discussing astrological signs and asked me when I was born. I said I was a Gemini, and one lady said, "Oh, that's an air sign."

"We know!" added the director, laughing. My face got really red, and not intentionally this time. Mom thought this was incredibly funny, and we would laugh about it for years, saying that maybe I should fart in auditions more often and I'd get more movie roles. Needless to say, the movie (later retitled again and rereleased as *Holy Terror*) was not a box-office hit but went on to become a bit of a cult classic.

Soon after filming *Alice, Sweet Alice,* I was brought in and cast by Woody Allen, to appear in a new movie he was directing that was titled *Annie Hall.* I was going to play the focus of the young Alvy's obsession. In one of the scenes I was a sexy pilgrim in a flashback of a Thanksgiving-themed school play. I filmed for only two days, and although singled out briefly, I was one of many kids in the scene. I did stand out because I was dressed all in white with flowing hair while the others had mismatched clothing and seemed uncomfortable. Woody had chosen every odd-looking child he was able to find in New York City. The scene was filmed in a gymnasium and we were all given box lunches. During this time my mother and I had adopted a husky puppy, and Mom had brought the dog to visit me for lunch. I didn't wish to finish my box lunch and asked Mom where I should put it. She said, "Give it to funny face."

I went to a little boy who was very short for his age, had black greasy hair flattened down on his head, and wore Coke bottle–thick glasses. I handed him my lunch. Mom blurted out, "I meant the dog!"

I felt so bad for having thought the kid was "Funny Face" and prayed his mother didn't hear the conversation. Thankfully, neither the kid nor the mom heard a thing. But, embarrassingly, Mom and I did laugh pretty hard about it later that day.

The strangest part about doing *Annie Hall* was that Woody Allen asked my mother out on a date and she went. I think it was only the one night and it was just dinner. Mom left the apartment, and our close friend Alice from across the street came to babysit. Alice was young and blond and like a big sister to me. While Mom was out, Alice and I made crazy-funny signs that said things like "Oooooh, how was your date?" Or "Did Woody get smoochy smoochy?" Or "Hope you had fun, Mom."

We stuck them all over the hallway on the seventh floor. When Mom got off the elevator, she was faced with all these funny signs leading to our apartment door at the far end of the hall. It turned out the date was uneventful. She explained that Woody was too neurotic and was in too much therapy for her liking. It is fitting that that was her take on the situation: a woman who would never fully be able to examine herself honestly, criticizing a man who appeared desperate to examine his neurosis. I get the phobic piece being unattractive in any person, but self-reflection, in my mind, is never a bad thing.

In the final cut of the movie, the flashback of the school play was edited out. My sexy pilgrim ended up on the cutting-room floor. I am pretty certain this had nothing to do with the date, but it was fun teasing my mom and accusing her of doing something that made Woody cut me from the film.

Mom and I were the closest when we were laughing. Our comedy and innate sense of timing created our deepest bond. We had the same sense of humor and it would carry us through many a difficult period. Mom kept her wit basically until the end.

Even though things didn't work out with Woody, Mom did have two other notable relationships at the time. The first was a man named Bob, whom she began dating on and off when I was about three. I don't think Mom was ever really attracted to him or was in love with him, but he was a very generous man who loved us very much and he embraced me fully. He worked in oil rigs and shared with us substantially. I think Mom accepted him as a temporary provider but never wanted to remarry. He was around — and a very strong source of support for me — for many of the more tumultuous years, when Mom's drinking escalated to disruptive heights.

Mom also met a man in Brazil one summer named Antonio Rius. We had traveled to Rio when I was two, but we went back to visit several times during my childhood. Their relationship was intense. She was never more beautiful or happier than when they were together. But he was separated (though not divorced) from his wife, who said he'd never see his children again if he left her to marry an American. Mom was devastated but said if he was the type of man who could abandon his kids to be with her, then he would not have been the man with whom she fell in love. She said she would wait for him . . . and she did.

During these years my parents had very different reactions to my growing career. My father was uncomfortable with my fame and was intent on its not being a part of my life with him. I know he didn't approve of my being a model or an actress and never went to see any of my movies. He liked my TV work better and in later years enjoyed watching me on the Bob Hope specials and then on *Suddenly Susan*. But back then he really wasn't comfortable with my other life as an actress and model. I remember once when we were taking the annual family photo, Dad stepped out and looked at me and said, "Now, Brookie, don't pose!"

I was embarrassed and hurt but would later understand his fierce desire to keep me "normal."

Even though my mother always believed in me and pushed me to take risks and never give up, she was also familiar with rejection and abandonment. She was concerned with how I'd deal with it. It wasn't that she discussed it with me on an emotional level; she just tried to prevent me from feeling pain and rejection from others. But, ironically, over the years and thanks to her continued drinking, she herself would end up abandoning me the most and causing me the most emotional pain.

But in the moment, she could be wonderful. Right around the time I was starting to make movies, my mother took me to see the musical *Grease*. It starred Adrienne Barbeau and Jeff Conaway. Our seats were close to the stage. They were the seats we could afford, and back then Mom told me the closer the seats the better — something I would later learn was not true. We had not planned it, but we were attending the hundredth performance of the original Broadway production. The preshow for *Grease* usually consisted of some fifties music and the DJ revving up the audience members and inciting them to clap and dance in their seats. To celebrate this particular show and momentous occasion, the producers decided to hold a Hula-Hoop contest. Any audience member could join in on stage. Mostly people from the *Grease* era — the actual fifties and sixties — began volunteering to enter. The prize for first place was a signed album, a chance to take photos with the cast, and an invite to their cast party celebrating their one hundred shows. I had never Hula-Hooped in my life but wanted desperately to meet the cast. I jumped up and raised my hand. Mom smiled and through a somewhat clenched mouth reminded me that I had never Hula-Hooped before. I didn't care. Mom was always supportive of anything I wanted to try, but this was the first time I had ever volunteered to do something completely foreign, and in front of a packed and rowdy theatre. This was a far cry from singing in the church basement. She was nervous for me but encouraged my participation and urged me on.

"I'm going up there."

"OK, then. Knock 'em dead."

Well, I went up on stage and was given a Hula-Hoop and began to wiggle as if my life depended on it. It was nine adults, who had been teenagers in the fifties and had Hula-Hooped many times before, and me. I was blindly determined. My jaw was set, I looked at no one, and I made no notice when a contestant dropped the hoop and was eliminated. Before long, it was down to one older man and me. I would not give up. My hoop would go all the way down, almost touching the stage, and then suddenly go all the way back up, each direction eliciting a different-toned "Wooooooo!" from the crowd.

My mom could not believe her eyes. Then, in one amazing moment that I did not even register, the old man's hoop dropped to the floor. I kept going until the DJ stopped me and said, "Well, little lady, we might need to make you a part of our cast! Congratulations, and I'll see you at the party."

I didn't even hear the thunderous applause. Back in my seat, the show began. From the overture till the finale, I was riveted. After the show I met the cast and got their signatures on my vinyl cast recording and attended the celebration. They presented me with a small trophy that said "Hula-Hoop Winner 1976." From that day on, if I ever expressed a fear of failure, my mom would simply say, "Remember the Hula-Hoop!"

■ ■ ■ ■

Part Two

■ ■ ■ ■

I've never left her as a daughter, but everytime she drinks and hurts me, she leaves me as a mother. It's been like this all my life.

— *Brooke's diary*

Part Two

CHAPTER FIVE:
PRETTY BABY

My mother never had any clear plans regarding a career path for her daughter. We kind of just kept rolling along with whatever came our way. One day I could be doing some print ad for the epidemic of young pregnancy and the next I could be doing an amazing ad for the inside of *Life* magazine, standing in a bathing suit next to Lisanne, a fellow model and close friend. I did some commercials and had two movies under my belt, but we had no idea if I was an actress, a model, or a spokesperson for good causes. As a side note, I feel that this multifaceted approach has always been both a blessing and a curse. I am in a business that loves to define and categorize talent. Being multifaceted suggests that there is a jack-of-all-trades-and-master-of-none quality. It has made for an interesting and extremely versatile career but at times has been strangely and frustratingly limiting.

But back when we were just beginning, each job meant Mom and I could buy something. As we worked and I earned, Mom and I began to be able to buy things like cars, homes, jewelry, or vacation trips. We went from job opportunity to job opportunity never really thinking in terms of how each project contributed to my career as a whole, or how it fit into the overall representation of me as a talent. Mom also never had specific goals that we reached for. Basically, the criteria for whether I took a job or not was this: Did it fit into my school schedule? Was it going to be a fun and different experience? Would it pay well?

I don't remember it ever really being about the type of film, or caliber of people involved, or even if a particular film or project propelled me into any particular category as a performer. Mom and I never considered if any one project made sense in the context of the future of my career. She never really considered nurturing my talent or pushing me to study acting. Rather, it seemed that success was measured in property and popularity.

Early on, it became evident that there were not many actresses who looked like I did. People kept saying that I had a unique look. As much as I was working in print, I still often didn't fit into the all-American type that was popular in TV and film. I was frequently turned down for not looking like a freckled-face kid from a farming town. I was still "too European."

How weird is it that I would eventually be labeled "America's sweetheart"? Did Mom consciously commit to changing these early impressions? I really don't think so. I certainly wasn't Shirley Temple, and although I had always been compared to Elizabeth Taylor, I had no *National Velvet* to identify me as the next "girl next door."

So when an acclaimed French filmmaker called me in to meet him for the lead role in his first American film, Mom thought I might have a fighting chance.

Why not? Mom loved European films and directors and had exposed me to films by Fellini and others. She seemed to understand the level of artistry they represented, and she always said women like Catherine Deneuve, Ingrid Bergman, and Sophia Loren were the classiest and most beautiful and most talented actresses out there. I also think she wished she resembled them a bit in style and stature and looks. Personally, I thought my mom was even prettier than any of them.

A meeting was arranged, and, thankfully,

Louis Malle was not interested in an all-American look for his star. The film was to be titled *Pretty Baby.* It told the story of photographer E. J. Bellocq, who became famous in the early 1900s for photographing women living and working in the bordellos of the red-light district in New Orleans. In this movie, based on his real life and real stories, he falls in love with a young prostitute, Violet, who had been born and raised inside one of these houses.

Meeting with Louis wasn't an audition in any typical way. We didn't work from a script. I went into an office somewhere in the middle of Manhattan and chatted with Louis Malle and the film's producer, Polly Platt. Polly and a guy named Tony Wade were the unit production managers. Polly had been married and divorced from director Peter Bogdanovich and was currently in a relationship with Tony.

I don't remember too much about the "audition," except that we spoke for quite some time. My mom was not a part of any of the conversation. She wasn't even in the room. I have always been under the impression that Mom never wanted to be thought of as a stage mother who hovered and interfered. She wanted to be the un–stage mother who was part of the team. In actuality, Mom was much more of an emotional hoverer who affected me internally.

However, I realize now that my mother was likely very distracted by what had happened much earlier that day. The night before, Mom had taken me and my model friend Lisanne out to a bar. Lisanne and I were very close friends and Mom always thought she was one of the most beautiful girls in the business. This particular night out, not only had we stayed out very late, but also Mom got pretty drunk. Lisanne spent the night but needed to be taken to Penn Station in the morning for a train back home. The next morning, Mom, still kind of tipsy from the previous night's imbibing, piled us in the black Jeep and drove to downtown Manhattan for my big movie meeting. Mom told me to go into the meeting room and she'd be back to get me. After basically leaving me with strangers, Mom left and took Lisanne to the station. Evidently she had two fender benders on the way, but Lisanne made her train. Mom came back to pick me up and didn't say a thing. I didn't know that it had happened at all until Lisanne told me years later.

But back in the room, I was having a wonderful time. The team showed me photos of inspiration for the film and I was completely enamored of the clothing and the culture of the period. It all seemed beautiful to me. Like an old-fashioned fantasy world.

The world seen through the eyes of E. J. Bellocq reminded me of paintings I had seen in museums my mom had taken me to. We chatted about the subject of the film. They asked me how I felt about a love story that takes place in a world of prostitution. I don't remember if they phrased it with such articulation, or as if they were talking to an adult, but I understood the gist of their question.

I replied that my mother had told me about the part and that I had already known about prostitution by living in Manhattan. Mom and I often talked about the different choices people make. I added that it always seemed sad to me that the prostitutes I saw on Forty-Second Street had to walk on the streets in all sorts of weather and did not have nice homes. My mom always said we should pray for them. I assumed it was because they did not have a safe place in which to live. In the movie the prostitutes all lived at home, which seemed a much more protected setting.

I don't remember if the question of nudity came up in the meeting, but I was later under the impression that my mom had discussed with the producers, and they had agreed on no explicit nudity. She was promised it would be filmed in a way that I would be protected. I honestly didn't give it any thought. I think I assumed that it would all be OK. Somehow I had no qualms about any of it. I was eleven. I'd go to the bathroom with the door open in front of people and have full-on conversations. I was not conscious of my body. Never young but somehow youthful.

Even though I was such a young girl, I always had mature and evocative looks. I was far from precocious, and that was what Louis Malle wanted. I was not in any way what Nabokov had called a nymphet or a Lolita. That wasn't what Louis Malle envisioned for his Violet. He believed that her power rested in her wise innocence. Louis wanted a sense of duality and contradiction in his lead character. He saw the woman/child as someone with real naïveté and innocence coupled with intelligence and emotional maturity. He didn't want savvy provocation. I was what he wanted — at once a little girl and an emotionally mature adult, all the while lacking shrewdness or a cunning persona.

The audition/meeting didn't last very

long. I was surprised it was so easy and fast. I worried that I should have done more. My mother picked me up and we left. As I remember it, we got the call later that same day. I was offered the role. Mom asked if I wanted to do the film and I said it sounded like a fun movie to make. We would get to move to New Orleans for a few months — we had thought it would be over summer vacation — and I'd get to dress up in period clothing. We would have a whole new adventure. We accepted the part.

Another reason Louis said he chose me was that I was not a trained actress. I had never studied acting, and he felt I would be able to just respond to situations once I understood the scene. This has always felt like the smartest approach to me.

Production was pushed back and what was supposed to be a summer shoot ended up starting around mid-February. This would be the first time I would miss school to work, but we had signed on and the money was good and this was a famous director. It was an opportunity not to be passed up. Mom and I felt we could make it work with a tutor and homework assignments. Plus, I knew in advance and could try to get ahead in school before leaving for New Orleans, which I was able to do.

The entire movie was shot in and around New Orleans. It had all been storyboarded and was seemingly meticulously planned out. The majority of the filming took place in a big white house on Saint Charles Avenue, which has since been converted into the Columns Hotel. The house had a big porch, a beautiful winding staircase, and stained-glass windows. Inside and out, the film's creative team built the world as it actually existed during E. J. Bellocq's time.

But once we arrived, everything was more chaotic than I imagined. The cast and crew were a rowdy bunch. They became known for their loud partying and drug usage. Every night, crew members would either take over the bar or use their rooms to party. Complaints from visitors would be lodged but never seemed to cause change. A lot went on and there were many on-set romances, including a pregnancy (my mother went with the poor girl when she had her abortion). We had all left our real lives at home and had entered a somewhat altered universe.

I enjoyed life on the set, but it could be very difficult and tense. There was a mystique surrounding Louis. He was making his first American film and there was a great deal of pressure, and he was often a man of few words. He watched more than he talked. He was not one to praise his actors. At first this scared me because I was like a Jack Russell puppy jumping up and up and up, asking, "Do you like me now? Do you like me now?" I wanted to do anything for a treat and a nod. Louis's reticence made me nervous, but I always believed he was kind.

He could be difficult with me but he was never mean or overtly demanding. I learned to navigate his often distant manner, and even though he seemed removed, I came to trust that no words were good words. I never fully knew whether he was ultimately happy with my portrayal of his lead character, but I had to believe he was getting what he wanted from me.

At times I craved more direction and felt awkward not being constantly told what to do and how to be and sometimes even how to feel. I began the movie by asking questions or if I was OK, but as time went on I, too, quieted and trusted my instincts a bit more. Sadly, this would be one of the last films in a long while during which I was learning my craft and experiencing hints of self-confidence. I believe it was because of the quality and artistic caliber of the director. He had vision and he expressed himself quietly and without unnecessary chatter.

He could say, "Just be defiant." I knew exactly what that meant to Violet.

The cinematographer, Sven Nykvist, was a genius. A gentle, beautiful soul whose art came out through his eyes and his heart. He was incredibly sweet and had a shy little laugh whenever I did or said something funny. I remember how quietly he worked and how thorough he was. If Louis was revealing what he called "a slice of life," then it was Sven who simultaneously stripped away facades and illuminated the honest truth.

We were all working long hours every day on the film, and sleep became my most coveted commodity. The amount of work I was required to do was staggering. The shooting days lasted between twelve and fifteen hours and included early calls, late wraps, and all-night shoots that began at 5:00 P.M. and went until at least 5:00 A.M. the next day. The weather was at times excruciatingly hot, and when we worked near the rivers the bugs ate us alive. Occasionally it was miserable, but none of us complained.

Because it was a period piece (my favorite thing in the world to do), all the costumes were authentically from the era. Nowadays many of the undergarments are remade in new materials, and shoes are copied in the style of the 1900s but with more comfortable modern technology. But on this film we were working with the legendary costume designer Mina Mittelman, and she had warehouses filled with period costumes. Her stock was plentiful and she was insistent that even the undermost petticoats be from the actual era.

I adored how beautiful the clothes looked but the shoes created a real problem for me. They were old and dry and I got a terrible case of an eczema-type rash that made my feet crack and bleed. I had waited to tell my mom how much they hurt and hoped it would get better on its own. I was never one to admit a discomfort and did not want to be a problem. There was work to get done and I could deal with the pain.

They were the shoes I had to wear the most, and when not wearing them, I was usually barefoot and running across broken shells. Neither option was a good one. The shells were used in the backyard to create a sort of driveway, so to protect me from getting badly cut, the wardrobe person taped moleskin to the bottoms of my feet. This helped and tickled when I peeled them off.

I never asked my mom to run lines with

me the night before; I was happy to memorize and do the work on my own. I liked hearing it in my own head before getting the input from anybody. This meant that I was experiencing much of the filming on my own and within my relationships with actors and the creative team on set. I loved having this entirely separate family and life to the one Mom and I lived together. It felt safe and fun and we all had a common goal.

But things began getting difficult and I was becoming run-down and tired. The schedule had been extended, and we were overbudget and tensions were high. Mom intervened and insisted that whenever my feet were not visible in the frame I could wear other shoes or go barefoot. She called a doctor and he prescribed a medicinal salve I was to use nightly. Mom would coat my feet in this ointment and then wrap them in bandages or athletic socks. Each morning it was a relief for them to be soft and a bit less cracked. My feet eventually healed, but Mom remained displeased that it had gone on for as long as it had and that nobody on set had bothered to address the issue. I had never told anybody else how bad it really was. I tried to explain that to her, but she said they still should have been more conscientious when using worn period items.

Up until this film my work environments had always been very controlled. We knew what to expect and Mom had been fine leaving me at a bit of a distance to do the job at hand. On this set she was more around, but contrary to popular belief, she was not always intruding; I never saw her giving her input to the director. She knew call times and locations, but I honestly felt she didn't want to interfere with the creative process.

Tensions were mounting between Polly Platt and my mother, and if it were up to Polly, Mom would have not set foot in New Orleans at all. Everybody wanted control of his or her own domain. When it came to me, my mom had no intention of relinquishing any. I was eleven years old.

I liked knowing Mom was near, and I was glad she intervened, but I never wanted her too close to me when I acted. I hated it when she watched me perform, and would get distracted if I saw her out of the corner of my eye. I never thought I was good enough, and her watching me would make me too nervous and I'd freeze. I felt I was good enough for basic strangers but feared my mother would be somehow dissatisfied. I was embarrassed and nervous about not being perfect for her. I just wanted her to think I was good, but I feared I might not be.

What was strange was that Mom always said she was proud of me and that in her eyes I was perfect, but she'd also make little comments that seemed like jokes or throwaways but made me feel less than. I couldn't get past the self-doubt and the insecurity of wanting to always be the best for her.

I am sure it made her feel sad and left out when I told her I didn't want her to watch me, but she found other ways to feel needed and important. I'm also sure Mom spent a good portion of her day drinking. She had a favorite bar she frequented during the days and nights and quickly became a regular. It was sort of near the St. Charles Hotel, and if I wrapped and the van dropped me off at the hotel and she was not there, I could usually find her at Igor's Lounge. Teri Terrific gravitated to seedy bars no matter where we were. She always had her favorites and loved being a regular. She often met our tall, slightly disheveled hippie of a boom operator at this famous bar they called "EE-EEYYYOORRRSS." His name was Ringo and he had an unkempt sex appeal about him. He was tall and had muscled arms from holding up the heavy boom all day. He was very sweet and protective of me and

I know Mom had a crush on him. I don't know if they ever hooked up. To be honest, I didn't want to know. It made me squeamish and jealous and angry just thinking about it.

Pretty Baby was based on a real story, and Violet was modeled after an actual person. The real Bellocq was rather unattractive, however, and was said to have had an enlarged head caused by hydrocephalus. (Obviously our version of Bellocq was the very handsome Keith Carradine.) It could have been because of his deformity that the girls in the brothel trusted him, but they also believed his intentions were pure. He was an artist with no ulterior motives who wanted only to capture the girls beautifully and with their individual personalities.

The still photos we took of the actresses were direct duplicates of the original Bellocq photographs and were remarkably similar. There was a scene, adapted from the actual historical photo, where Violet's image was being taken while she lay naked on a chaise lounge. I had been given a G-string, but it was determined by all of us that it wasn't necessary. My legs were slightly crossed and Louis did not want it to be pornographic in any way. The shot was quick and represented the snap of Bellocq's lens right before my character jumps up to petulantly destroy some photo plates.

We copied the famous photo and I was unself-conscious and unfazed by what was an extremely short scene. I remember only being slightly disappointed that I had no real breasts yet, but neither did the young girl on the photo plate. I didn't feel violated or compromised. I put the G-string back on once I was standing and was also only photographed from the shoulders up. I had not yet learned how to use my sexuality as any type of tool and was therefore able to play this scene with the calm quality it called for.

Mom again didn't watch the filming of this scene and no one seemed to fret. It was quick and I was so young and innocent. Mom was crucified for permitting any of it, and in many ways I understand the criticism, especially now that I'm a mother. But the world and the industry were markedly different back then.

I have been asked this question over and over in the press, but I have always maintained that, at the time of the filming and thereafter, I did not experience any distress or humiliation. When the movie came out a year later, the press was up in arms about the whole thing. There was a sense of fury and a need to assume that I was a victim in this circumstance. The press wanted me to have shame and regret and could not handle my being cognizant and wise and self-possessed. There was a firestorm and Mom took most of the heat. My poise, whether innate or earned, gave me a certain adult perspective, and I remained clear in my convictions of the scene and of the film in its entirety.

As a mother of an eleven-year-old today, I am equally clear that I, myself, would not allow my daughter to be photographed topless. But it was a different time, and not only did my mother really believe we were creating art, but this film was special, too, and the scene was one of the shortest ones in the entire film.

I was not yet a sexual being, and this was how Louis Malle wanted it to be. He was more interested in showing my emerging sexuality through my attitude rather than via gratuitous nudity. We simply did not make a big deal of it. I was never scarred in the way the press wanted to speculate and hope.

I was, however, deeply concerned by a much more innocuous scene. Later in the film, once Violet and Bellocq have gotten to know each other a bit better, they're playing a game they call "sardines" and find themselves alone in an attic and kiss for the first time. During the filming, I kept scrunching up my face right before a first kiss. Louis kept saying "Cut" and I could tell he was getting slightly disturbed. He wanted it to look tender and beautiful, not like I had just sucked on a lemon. All of a sudden Keith, who played Bellocq, whispered to me, "You know it doesn't count, right?"

"It doesn't?"

"Of course not, it's fake."

This was the first time I had ever kissed anybody on the lips except my mother, and I was so relieved that it would not count as my first kiss that I totally relaxed and the scene went on without another hitch. In hindsight, I feel that the director, or at least my mother, should have shared this sort of insight with me before Keith had to do it. I was very lucky that Keith was so kind. He was such a gentleman and was lovely to both my mother and me. I am sure he was struggling by having to film romantic scenes with a young girl, but he showed me such gentle respect that it made it all easy.

I would not be quite as lucky when it came to Susan Sarandon, who played my mother,

Hattie. Hattie and Violet had a difficult relationship, and the scenes Susan and I had together were very challenging. Her attitude toward me ran the gamut, and while she could be sweet to me off set, she sometimes approached me during filming in a manner that seemed to cross a line. It would always be in the guise of staying true to her character but also hinted at something I did not quite understand. Now, she was extremely talented and beautiful and maybe she was just really being a serious actress who chose to stay in character for the duration of the film, but there were inconsistencies in this theory.

My mother seemed to understand early on that there might be some discomfort between Susan and me. Mom actually warned me that there might be some jealousy between us. I didn't get it. Susan was young and very sexy, and it was obvious Louis liked her. Why would she have a problem with eleven-year-old me? But I will admit that I felt something was up. Something was uncomfortable and I got the feeling she did not like me very much. I am almost positive she would not interpret any of it this way, but it was a vibe I was constantly trying to navigate.

Mom hinted that Susan may have been

threatened by me because I was the lead in the film. In addition, it turned out that even though it was not yet public knowledge, everybody on set knew that Susan and Louis were involved in a romantic relationship.

Susan was breaking up with her then-husband, Chris Sarandon, and would be divorced within two years. I don't remember how Mom alluded to this, but where Mom lacked in maternal advice, she seemed to make up for with regard to a woman's mind and her actions. Mom was pretty intuitive when it came to other people's internal emotions. Which was funny, since she usually wasn't particularly in touch with her own.

One day we were filming a scene in which Hattie tells her daughter that she is getting married to a respectable man and leaving her daughter behind, at least temporarily. She has told her fiancé that Violet is her sister so he would marry her. Violet stands stoically, and instead of commenting, she just cocks her head, raises her eyes slightly, and smugly offers her mother some lemon custard she had been eating from a little bowl with her index finger. Hattie immediately and violently slaps her daughter across the face. The slap conveyed so much.

Before shooting the scene, Susan explained to Louis that she would be unable to fake the slap. She would have to actually slap me in order to act her most convincing. She literally said, "I can't do this unless I actually slap her."

I remember thinking: *Is this being a real actress, or does she really not like me? Oh, well, I'll show her she can do what she wants. She won't hurt me.*

It was in this scene that Louis's direction to me was simply to be "defiant." In any case, I decided to act as if I couldn't care less what she did. So I stood there and took repeated slaps across my left cheek without flinching. I remember feeling stubborn and resilient and that I was showing her how she couldn't affect me. This reacting was also telling and was equally appropriate for Violet and for Brooke. There was something hurtful yet empowering about standing up to her in this way and in response to her trying to rule how the scene went. It was perfect for the scene, so maybe Susan did this on purpose, but I'll never know.

The funny thing is that in truth, although seemingly polarized in life, Violet and I were not that different. I had been supporting my mother's sometimes distant or angry attitude with a similar approach for years.

When Mom drank, she would get flippant, and hurtful verbal attacks were not uncommon. Nasty barbs and inappropriate insults could fly out of her mouth without warning. I often chose to remain stoic and unaffected by her change in behavior. She would often impatiently bark orders at me to "sit up" or "say thank you" or "don't do that" or "God, Brookie, wise up." "Move your ass. Stop being such an ingrate."

I actually learned to thrive by adopting the attitude of "I don't care, you can't hurt my feelings." As Violet, I summoned a jaw-jutting, smug, steely gaze that felt very familiar from real life.

It took a minimum of nine takes from each angle to complete the coverage on this scene. Oddly enough, I got a smidgen of a payback when I saw the finished movie. As I closely watched this scene on film, I noticed red finger marks on my cheek from a previous take. This may have been wrong for the film, but I felt privately avenged.

This particular incident excluded, for the majority of the time, everybody involved with the making of *Pretty Baby,* including Susan, treated me quite well and with genuine kindness. But, as time went on, and the movie went overbudget, things got more intense. I always felt Mom was there to protect me against whatever threats existed.

My mother and Polly Platt had begun as friends, but this friendship rapidly deteriorated. Polly and Tony were at the helm of a ship that had found itself in troubled waters, and they would stop at nothing to get their film made.

The long hours started really getting to me, but I still would never complain. I was never a quitter and would keep that proverbial Hula-Hoop up around my waist for as long as necessary. Mom began outwardly commenting that she couldn't believe a minor was being allowed to work as much as I was working. I had made only one small independent movie and Mom and I were still relatively new to the film industry. We had no idea how big studio movies were made. She made a call to the local labor board to find out their rules regarding working minors. She was just trying to get basic information and find out what the local laws were. As a model in New York City, there were some protections for models, but not many, and nothing like those protecting TV and film actors. I was already a member of SAG because of my first movie, so we thought the same protection that was provided elsewhere had to apply in this case.

But, because I was a New York hire and not a Louisiana hire, they led us to believe that the same rules didn't apply to me. The producers were hiring mostly union actors for their film, but they wanted to work them as much as they needed to complete the project, so they just kept stretching the rules. That was until my mom began sniffin' around. She had no idea what rock she had just overturned.

Apparently the union that represented the film's crew was working together with the local authorities and therefore also "collaborating" with New Orleans organized crime. The powers that be got wind of Mom's call and spread the word that my mother was trying to shut down production. This wasn't true, but they wanted to put a stop to anything that threatened to delay the filming of this overbudget and overdue film.

As I remember it, the night after Mom called the labor board, she and I returned to our hotel room to find the lock had been broken and the door left ajar. In my adjoining bedroom, written in Mom's red lipstick on the mirror over the dresser, were the words: *This is to let you know what we can do!*

The next day, when we picked up the

room phone we heard clicking on the line. Mom said she feared the lines were being tapped. I had no idea what that meant, and when she explained that somebody might be listening to our conversations, I immediately thought only of my potential romantic life. I became terrified my calls to the Bodack boys back home would be listened to. Naïvely, I didn't know there was anything else to fear.

Mom had befriended the cleaning lady in this hotel and showed her the writing on the mirror. The woman said that there was clearly something going on in the producer's room because she would find blood splatters and needles in the garbage baskets. Outwardly, Mom seemed unruffled, and I continued to work the long hours. Mom had a plan, though. Mafia or no mafia, drugs or no drugs, she was going to do something about it. Whoever was causing trouble didn't know my mother.

But the opposition was ready to play dangerously dirty. One day my mother took the same hotel cleaning lady out to lunch for her birthday. Mom drove to meet her on her day off from the hotel. They went to a restaurant off a highway a bit away from town and had a celebratory birthday lunch. After the conclusion of lunch, both women got into their cars and began the drive back. My mom was driving a rental, and as she entered the highway, she lost control of the car. The brakes failed and she swerved and was only able to slow the car on a truck incline. Mom told me that within seconds, a patrol car's lights began flashing and a cop was out of his car approaching my mom. There was no doubt that Mom drank during lunch, but it was a sad (and unfortunately true) fact that my mother was capable of driving drunk and avoiding being pulled over for being beyond her limit. There was something suspicious about her losing control of the vehicle and how quickly the cops arrived. It was as if the cops had been waiting for her and they weren't the only parties involved. Something seemed suspicious about all of it. Mom was arrested on the spot for drunk driving and was taken to a holding cell at the police station.

From the cell Mom called her lawyer in New York City immediately. Being a tough broad who could fight, Mom and her lawyer came up with a plan to deal with how we were being treated. She had only a lucky nickel she kept in her Levi's minipocket but decided to save it for now. She decided to call a friend from the set and reverse the charges, asking the friend to tell me that she was fine but that she would not see me tonight. Mom then used the actual nickel to call my French tutor, who was also on set, to come and bail her out.

All I remember is this friend telling me to come directly to her room in the hotel after work and not to tell anybody where I was going. It all seemed kind of exciting to me and I played along. In the room I spoke to Mom on a phone that had evidently not been tapped. She told me that some people were not happy with the fact that Mommy had had lunch with the black cleaning lady and that something strange had happened to her car. She said laws were different down in New Orleans and it would all be OK. She insisted I not let anybody know where I was but to report to work as usual the next day. Now, she was not wrong about the racial tension in New Orleans at the time, but something quite big was going down and she wanted to spare me the truth.

Mom was going back to New York for a few days. I loved Mom's friend and welcomed a sleepover. I had no idea what was really going on. At one point I remember somebody banging on the hotel door. I hid in the tub and Mom's friend opened the door. Someone — it may have been Tony Wade — asked if she had seen me. She calmly replied no. I remained undetected, had some room service, and went to bed. The next morning, at call time, I went down to the lobby as usual.

The moment I got off the elevator, Tony was waiting for me. He quickly hustled me into the stairwell, and on the cold, gray metal stairs, he very seriously looked me in the eye and said: "Your mother has been in a very serious accident. There was a lot of blood and you may never see her again."

Somehow I knew it was time to be defiant again. Head slightly cocked, with a slightly curious scowl on my forehead, I said, "Oh, that's funny because I spoke to her and she sounded fine, so if you'll excuse me, I have to get to work."

I don't know if I was channeling Violet at that moment, but I didn't like Tony Wade anyway, and I loved knowing I was doing what my mom needed and that we were a team. I was unflappable and enjoyed being a good soldier.

I continued filming while Mom remained in New York for a few days. During this time she managed to get a mechanic friend to come check out her vehicle. He deduced that the brakes on my mother's car had undoubtedly been manually cut, and that the whole thing was a setup.

After Mom returned from New York, things changed for me. First of all, we moved out of the St. Charles Hotel and into the Fairmont Hotel, which was a beautiful old hotel in the downtown area of New Orleans. It was safe and quiet, and because we were separated from the rest of the crew, it meant fewer parties. It was, however, closer to Igor's and therefore easier for my mother to stop in for a nip more often. I tried to look on the bright side by justifying that it was also easier for me to find Mom on those nights she went missing for a bit. It was a beautiful, fancy hotel, and I honestly don't think Mom picked it for its proximity to booze, but I wouldn't put it past her.

Suddenly I wasn't working such long hours and I had more breaks on set in which to study. Things got so much better for me that I remember frequently feeling guilty. I even felt kind of like I was missing out by not working the same hours as everyone else. I loved being with these people, even if it meant all day and night. They had become my family. Even when we were waiting on the light or moving locations, I wanted to play games with them and enjoy our inside jokes. Sometimes it was sticking a KICK ME sign on a big gaffer's back, or doing arts and crafts with the wardrobe people, but it felt like home. I loved the actresses and would entertain them on the big porch of the white house by singing Barbra Streisand's "Queen Bee." The girls loved it, and Mom loved that they loved me. One day I wasn't called in until later in the day, but I got up and ready to go anyway. My mom said I did not have to go in.

"Oh, but I have to, Mama."

"Why?"

"Because I am their bubble."

I found out later that Mom had been able to alert the proper people and fix the situation legally, so I would actually get the benefits that I was meant to by being a member of SAG. I remember a welfare worker–type person being brought in and the tone on set changing. Production was on alert and no longer allowed to abuse the rules as they had been for almost three months.

The production company was less than overjoyed by this new state of affairs and I am sure it made my mother even more unpopular with Polly and Tony. But it worked. Thankfully for everyone, we only had about a month's worth of filming left for completion of the movie, and I don't remember these rules adding any days to the schedule.

I enjoyed my new freedom, but not fully. It was too much of a change and I felt isolated. I kind of wanted to let the crew bend the rules at times, and I'd beg the teacher to let me stay on set to finish an uncompleted sequence, but she rarely complied. We all wanted to get this movie finished.

Finally, the wrap was upon us. The last day of filming was surreal. This had been my first starring role in a film. I loved the feeling of being part of a film family and I had grown very attached to everyone involved. I was even, in a way, attached to Polly and Tony. Something happens when you share an experience with people. A bond is created, and whether it's a positive or negative experience, connection is made. Because of my youth and maturity I bonded easily.

The day we shot our last shot, the cast and crew erupted with applause and hugs. It was the applause of collective relief. Four months of hard work, tears, pain, fear, insecurities, and rough conditions. We had survived together. We had created something we all felt was important.

At the wrap party, back at the St. Charles

Hotel, my mom asked me what I wanted as a wrap gift. I said I wanted to cut my hair all off. I wanted a haircut partially because my hair had been destroyed during the making of the film with irons and teasing and techniques that were used to make it look frizzy and of the era. My main reason, however, was that I thought that if I chopped off all my hair, they would not be able to call me the next day and say we had reshoots or a scene had been added. As sad as I was that it was over, I was so relieved that I did not have to actually film anymore. I wanted to make sure that I would be unable to, if called. My mom gave me money then and there and said I could go do what I wanted.

"Surprise me," she said.

I was thrilled with that freedom and went to a local salon. I told the woman to cut it all off and she gave me a shapeless bob. I really didn't care what my hair looked like. To me it was liberating to be able to turn my head from left to right and have my hair swing back and forth past each shoulder. I was excited about how light and released I felt. This was a seeming act of rebellion and I felt freed. I would not follow up this act in any way for decades.

Two days after we wrapped, Mom and I

boarded a plane to New York. I cried the entire plane ride "home." I instantly missed everyone and felt I had not said good-bye to everyone enough. It felt like a death. I had never felt more disoriented or homesick in my life. I was confused by my feelings but knew they were quite real. Going back into the real world and my real life would be like reentering Earth's atmosphere after going to outer space.

Once in New York City I couldn't shake my depression. Mom tried to comfort me by saying we would keep in touch with people, but somehow I knew that would not be the case. I felt drained and tired and a bit confused. Together, Mom and I made the decision that we were done. I would not be filming any more movies. The entire experience, and the toll it took to endure and then readapt to real life, was too much to take.

CHAPTER SIX:
FUCK 'EM IF THEY CAN'T HANDLE IT

Once I returned to New York it was time to go back to school. This year I was starting junior high in a brand-new school. I had only attended schools so far on the Upper East Side. I had gone to the Everett School through the second grade until it closed. From third through sixth grade I went to the Lenox School. It was an all-girls school and would stay that way until 1974. It was a wonderful school and academically superior to my next school.

Mom, however, did not want me to continue at an all-girls school because she said she believed it was important for girls and boys to be friends and not socially intimidated by one another. I adored Lenox and still have a friend I hold dear to my heart from those years. But Mom insisted. The natural progression for me — especially because my dad was paying my tuition — was for me to go to a Spence, Brearley, or

Chapin, all legendary and traditional girls' schools, but Mom wanted me to have a coed education. So after wrapping *Pretty Baby* and right after returning to New York, I enrolled at the New Lincoln School. New Lincoln was a coed school known for its diversity. I remained there and floundered for two years. We had no uniforms and the curriculum was characteristic of the seventies.

Going to a new school was both a relief and in ways frightful. The frightful part came first in the form of a pair of gauchos. Because I was attending a school that did not require uniforms, a first for me, I needed practically an entirely new wardrobe. Mom took me shopping and we picked out clothes that would be fitting for a school in England. She took me to thrift shops for my clothes and proceeded to amass a wardrobe of wool vests, tweed jackets, corduroy gauchos, plaid skirts, white shirts, and of all things . . . dickies! She might as well have included a cabby hat.

I followed her lead, as usual, and got excited about looking smart and stylish for my first day of school. I chose the gauchos and a white shirt and vest, finished off with penny loafers. I walked proudly into my first day of seventh grade in an outfit straight out of the musical *Newsies.* I took one look at the jeans-clad, ripped-T-shirt-wearing hippie kids and wanted to run. I couldn't believe Mom let me go to this school dressed like I should have been on a street corner yelling out headlines. I was so embarrassed and mad that when I got home I said I looked stupid and that everybody made fun of me, and I refused to wear any of the clothes Mom bought me ever again. She didn't fight me and even bought me the Frye boots I eventually begged for and wore almost every day. I'd tuck my blue jeans into my Frye boots and I finally fit in.

During this time Mom and I began putting together a book called *The Brooke Book,* which consisted of photos of me, my writings and poetry, and various tidbits about my mother's prized baby girl. She worked on the book with her longtime friend John Holland, who was a hairdresser in the city. I loved John and laughed a lot with him. He and Mom believed I was "special" and that a book about me would actually sell. They worked on it a while, found a publisher, Pocket Books, and planned to release it around the time *Pretty Baby* hit the theatres.

The first few months of school, I made some very good friends but I struggled in my classes. The school was way too progressive for me, and the kids were much more mature. We were still living on Seventy-Third Street and I would walk to school every day with my mother. Just like the years before, mornings with my mother, before she started drinking, were once again the best times. She would pick me up in the afternoons, and the moment I looked at her face, I could tell. She'd look at me as if I were accusing her of doing the exact thing that she was doing. But I didn't have the guts to say this to her on the walks to school because I didn't want to ruin the one time a day I knew she would be most lucid. Even a hangover was a welcome relief from who she was when she drank.

Enough time had passed and the negative parts of *Pretty Baby* had all but been forgotten. I remained sought after for movies. I soon got an offer to be in a movie called *Tilt* starring Charles Durning. I would be playing a young pinball whiz who runs away from home to gamble by playing pinball.

Even though my mother and I had sworn I was done with movies, some time had passed and this project could not have seemed more different from *Pretty Baby* in terms of tone, time period, and duration of filming — only a few weeks in November and December 1977. Plus, this one sounded fun and we could use the money. But was it the right move for me, careerwise? My mother had no real long-term plan for my career, nor did she consider the quality of the projects or the directors. She appreciated the beauty of *Pretty Baby* but seemed unable to turn down projects just because they didn't carry the same artistic weight.

Did it not occur to her that following up a movie of the caliber of *Pretty Baby* with one being guided by a first-time American director might not have been such a smart move? There didn't seem to be a great deal of thought put into any of it beyond the question of money and the possibility of adventure. It seemed that my mom made many of my career choices based on everything but the creative factors.

To this day I remain shocked at her lack of commitment to craft. She truly had exquisite taste in the cinema we watched, but those parameters never seemed to consistently apply to me and the work I was doing or could be doing.

This absence of commitment to becoming a cultivated actor was perpetuated and supported over the years. It was easy to do because I was always busy working on something, so we could justify that I was successful and getting better. Two prominent film directors hired me because they did not want a studied thespian but an untapped resource. I had been labeled a "raw talent." Was raw talent supposed to become "studied"? Wouldn't that contradict the situation? And yet how was it supposed to be nurtured? Mom did not have a clue.

When working with directors like Louis Malle or, later, Franco Zeffirelli, I would trust them completely to spend time actually directing me. I knew they would not finish a scene until they were satisfied.

Later, I thought that because I knew I wanted to be an actress, Mom's goal was for me to be a cultivated one. She convinced me that work led to work and it would all come together, but I believe people became confused as to what I was. In high school, while I was dreaming of being in Merchant Ivory movies, Mom seemed to have had little focus beyond keeping me in the public eye and maintaining a name the world knew. I think Mom's goal was for me to be a movie star and for us to earn enough money to be wealthy. Fame to her was not a bad thing but it opened doors. She associated it with power. We both worked very hard for the money we had but not for the clarity of a career.

I am rather conflicted by it all. I appreciate that my work did not take precedence over my young life. Yet this attitude also seemed to keep me from committing to my work in a way imperative for growth and to cause a lack of clarity as to what I really was.

As a result, I never researched or deeply contemplated the characters I played, either. I learned my lines right before bed the night before and sometimes even on the day. I have a photographic memory, so memorization came easily. Mom never discussed the lives of the characters I portrayed. I never studied acting or took it very seriously. The moment the director yelled "Cut," I would jump out of character and back into silly kid-Brooke mode. I resented scenes in which I had to feel deep emotion. I wanted to pretend but not actually be affected by the emotions.

This was in a way healthy for a girl my age with my acute innocence but would take a toll on my talent. I just didn't take any of it too seriously. I thought all the actors who moped around or stayed in character all day were missing out on the fun it was to make movies.

But in the end, I feel my talent suffered. It would not be until years later that I recognized that I deeply wanted to be an actress and that I saw the beauty in identifying with the characters I played. My focus shifted slowly toward wanting to improve my ability. As I grew older, being respected for the quality of my work became my priority. As I matured, it all became a matter of perspective and balance. Whereas I had previously thought it a waste of time and embarrassing, I began to value the deeper levels of acting. I found freedom in detaching from everything to focus on a character. This would not happen until years later, however.

But back in 1977, I was too young to think in terms of a creative next move filmwise. But the sound of spending two months in sunny Santa Cruz, where I'd be eating Butterfingers and playing pinball, sounded a lot better than staying in New York, getting C's on tests, and being still somewhat socially awkward. Plus, I'd heard I'd have two pinball machines in the house we'd rent. It sounded like a vacation. I reconsidered my original position of never again doing another movie.

It's funny how Mom's stringent rules on my missing school changed just as I was entering my most important years of education. Just when my actual presence in school should have mattered, Mom decided that it made sense to leave for a few months at a time. But I didn't mind — I wasn't doing that well in my classes anyway! On set I would have a social worker and a tutor and I could get my assignments from my school. It might even be a positive thing, almost like being homeschooled. In addition, as an A-plus student in ACOA (Adult Children of Alcoholics), the only class in which I seemed to currently excel, I was secretly hoping that being away from New York would inspire my mother to curb the booze. Oh, how I continued to hang on to that persistent dream.

Mom and I packed up and headed out to Santa Cruz, California, and settled into a big wooden ranch-style house on a quaint street. Inside the living room sat the promised two pinball machines. One was Bally and the other a Williams. I was thrilled. I played during every free moment I had and became quite good. I had the mechanic set my tilt feature to be very delicate so as to make the game harder for me. I started to get very competitive but it was never against anybody else. I was always going up against my highest score.

I'd practice and practice, but at the time I had a bad temper in general and had always been a sore loser. I hated not winning, and if I made what I considered a stupid mistake, I often took it out on the machine. I once got so mad at myself for not playing well that I smashed my flat hands on the surface of the machine and screamed. Can anyone say "projection"?! Mom got so angry at me for displaying such a temper that she sent me directly to bed.

Even then I found it funny how conventional ways of parenting seemed so ill fitting on Mom. She typically didn't just ground me or send me to my room. No, she'd pour Yoo-hoo down the toilet or wake me up in the middle of the night and get me out of bed for no real reason. And on this particularly frustrating pinball evening, that was her exact punishment of choice. After sending me to my room, she continued to drink with friends, then suddenly decided to wake me up and force me into the living room. By now it was extremely late and I had fallen asleep on the top bunk of the dark-painted pine bunk bed. She threw open the door and told me to come out *now.* She told me to sit on the brown velvet couch in the living room and stare at the pinball machine. She wouldn't allow me to play but made me just sit there, looking at it and thinking about how not to get so angry. Well, this just made me angrier, quite honestly. It felt crazy to me, but I admittedly never smashed my hands on top of the machine again. Once more Mom's behavior was reinforced.

Mom prided herself on her particular methods. She practically gloated at the fact that she never spanked me. She preferred controlling my mind and my emotions. She honestly believed it was a genius approach and effective in ways that quick physical punishments weren't. She thought she was really doing the best thing for me. Simply discussing things might have been a nice change of pace. Mom also found that instilling the fear of potential punishment proved effective. I never got the belt, but she often left a wooden spoon on the kitchen counter where I could easily see it. Every now and then she would pick it up and smack the palm of her hand with it so it made a loud cracking sound. Each time I went near the spoon, I offered to put it away for her.

"I put away for Mommy?"

"Nah, that's OK. You can leave it out."

It was never unclear as to who held the power in my house. As I got older I sometimes wished I had been hit in order to be done with it. But I knew Mom would never hit me — she knew it would be wrong, and it wasn't in her nature to be violent. It could be in her nature to be nasty and hurtful and to emotionally unravel — but not to be physically violent. Mom would sooner come at me wielding a butter knife than a sharp one, dramatically crying about what I had done to her. I think Mom wanted to prove her prowess as an authority by manipulating my brain, not by hurting my body. She was creating and forming me and I was dutiful.

But back on set, filming was a lot of fun, but much to my dismay, Mom did not show any signs of quitting drinking. She treated the movie like a permission slip to drink. She drank and I played pinball all the time. We worked mostly in and around Santa Cruz and then went to various locations in Texas. We traveled to Corpus Christi and heard country music (my all-time favorite at the time), and I even got to ride the mechanical bull at Gilley's Club in Houston.

This was a great couple of months and not a great movie. I can't say I really cared. We had had another very different experience. I returned to school in January a very different student. It turned out that tutoring was immensely positive. Not only was I ahead of my class when I returned, but my study and organization skills had improved dramatically, too. Despite the fact that

Mom's drinking didn't get any better while we were gone, and she showed the first signs of how truly volatile she could be, I'd had a good time and we both had a better taste in our mouths concerning filmmaking. Once home, I again tried to forget how difficult it could be when Mom drank. Every shift in location seemed to give me hope. Back then I didn't know how irrational that sort of thinking was. I just craved what I felt was the safety net and avoidance tool a movie set was.

By the spring I had another movie offer. I was called in to meet Italian producer Dino De Laurentiis, who was producing a movie called *King of the Gypsies.* The film was a family drama about present-day Gypsies in New York and the reluctant rise to power of the eldest son. I was playing Susan Sarandon and Judd Hirsch's daughter. Shelley Winters and Sterling Hayden were my grandparents, and Eric Roberts played my brother. The director was Frank Pierson, who had written the Oscar-winning screenplay for *Dog Day Afternoon.* The movie shot in New York City and I had to film only during April and May of 1978. Because of the large cast, I had a very light shooting schedule and much less pressure than had I been the star. In hindsight, this was a good next step in my career. The cast was strong. It was a big Paramount production and had a reputable Italian producer at the helm.

I was a bit surprised that both Susan and I were cast as Gypsies because we both had very light coloring and sandy hair. She was completely lovely to me during this experience and I think she actually liked me. I was a bit older this time and clearly not the star. We were not isolated on a location together, and it was a totally different experience. We also never had a one-on-one scene together like the traumatic slapping incident during *Pretty Baby.*

It was rather cool to cast us as mother and daughter twice, because it almost seemed as if it were true. (The craziest thing is that now I would be too old to play her daughter. I'm not sure how I caught up, but now it almost looks like it.) Susan actually dyed her hair black for the film but Mom insisted on a Roux rinse for me. It was a temporary color that washed out. Every time I stood in the shower to wash my hair, the black dye would blanket the tub. I was glad not to have to dye my hair black, and I read later that Susan resented actually changing her hair color while I was allowed to use a temporary one.

I have to admit that her hair looked much more natural than mine did, and in hindsight, I feel her choice was the better one. Here again Mom made a choice that may have protected me personally but that compromised the integrity of the piece and my portrayal. It doesn't feel right to blame her. It frustrates me, but can I really say I'm angry now because she wouldn't let a production team do anything they wanted to my naturally highlighted blond-brown hair? It is interesting where she chose to draw the line, however. Consistency, except in drinking, was never one of my mother's strong points.

Shelley Winters was also fair skinned and lighter haired. She was a piece of work to navigate. I am not sure she liked me too much, but I can't say I liked her, either. We had only a few scenes together, so I knew I would survive. However, there was one scene in which my character was skateboarding through the hallways of the hospital as my grandfather lay dying in bed. I was supposed to be eating a sandwich that Shelley was going to rip out of my hand as I skated by. She insisted I eat ham on white Wonder Bread with ketchup. Who eats ham with ketchup?

I was the one who had to eat almost all of

it, and Shelley was just supposed to take it from me and have a bite. I hated ham and ketchup. But I couldn't complain because she was an Academy Award–winning actress. Take after take I ate that disgusting sandwich, not ever being told that I could spit it out once the director yelled cut. I had not learned many of the tricks, such as asking for a bucket near you to spit in once the camera had stopped rolling. I was getting sicker and sicker each take, but Miss Winters insisted that she could not act the scene unless it was a ham-and-ketchup sandwich on untoasted white bread. Slight flashback to *Pretty Baby,* but at least this time I was a moving target. I vowed never to do that to somebody else when I grew up. I never let on how sick I felt but passed on lunch that day.

Something dangerous and shocking happened while filming the final scene of the film. Eric Roberts's character saves me from my fate in the family by kidnapping me and driving away with me in his car. A wild and violent car chase ensues.

It was very late at night and the rain had just stopped. Right before we shot the scene, the stunt coordinator told me it might be a good idea to buckle my seat belt. Before Standards and Practices insisted that for legal reasons seat belts had to be shown fastened, we shot scenes unbuckled all the time. I found this recommendation from the stunt guy a bit strange but followed his advice.

We planned on driving and filming continuously down one long road. There was really no place set up for people to watch, so only the very necessary people were involved in the filming of this sequence. It was just the director, cameraman, Eric, and me in the car. The director was crouched down in the backseat to listen to the scene. The chase began and we accelerated to eighty miles per hour — easily — in just a few seconds as the other car began to gain on us and drift over to the passenger side. I have no idea if it was planned, but all of a sudden Eric wrenched the wheel to the right and slammed our car into a car speeding next to us. This happened repeatedly and on both sides of the cars. He began smashing into whatever side was closest to him. We smashed into the other car so hard each time that my side of the car dented in on me and I was bruised and terrified. We suddenly came to a halt, and our vehicle was so destroyed that the director's door was bent shut, and to free him they needed to radio for a Jaws of Life. I was shaking and crying and begged the director not to have to do the shot over again. Well, we couldn't even if he had wanted a second take because we had only these two cars.

I was shocked and scared that it had happened because up until then I assumed I'd always be safe on a movie set. Eric was not a stuntman and was not supposed to have done this stunt entirely on his own. We could all have been killed, and I was hurt that it had been allowed to be so real.

Today that would have caused quite a stir and legal actions would be taken, but they all just thought the scene was amazing. Because Mom couldn't watch the scene from anywhere, I think she must have been either back at base camp or at a bar. When I told her what had happened, I am sure she must have gotten upset, but I don't remember if she spoke up or not. This was very different from the way she acted during *Pretty Baby.* She must have been drinking much more during this movie to have let this incident slide. I am surprised that she did not make a big deal out of something that had resulted in a much more dangerous situation than long workdays or cracked feet.

Mom sometimes had small roles in my movies. In *King of the Gypsies* Mom played a hooker who leaves a party on Eric Roberts's arm. They stumble out of the building and stagger arm in arm down the dark street. Mom had to get drunk before she could do it. She never seemed to do anything pressured or important without drinking first. I remember thinking that Mom would have probably dated Eric. She was that sexy, boozy blond who flirted. She had a sharp wit and a provocative vocabulary. There seemed to be some guy on every set who had a crush on my mom and ended up asking her out. She managed to keep the details from me, and I never saw her be overtly romantic with anybody. I imagine she met people from the crew later after I was asleep. I hated anybody she had a crush on and she knew it.

The crash scene was one of my last on the film and I wrapped earlier than most. Soon the rest of the film was complete. We had a big wrap party at Regine's on Park Avenue. But something even more exciting was about to happen — within days we were on our way to the Cannes Film Festival. It was to be my first trip to France.

Pretty Baby premiered at the Cannes Film Festival and received the Palme d'Or. The film created a frenzy at Cannes. One that would scar me for life. The press both ripped us apart and could not get enough of the controversial nature of the movie. Certain members of the press called it pornography. I was being called the next Lolita. The very thing that Louis wanted to avoid was rearing its ugly head.

I was shocked and overwhelmed at people's reaction to me. The fans and press went insane. During the premiere of the film — before it won the award — the crowd was so big and disorderly that I was almost trampled. I was walking in flanked by my mother; her "companion," Bob; and some guards. Mom was holding on tightly to my arm as we pushed through the immense crowd. Out of the corner of my eye I saw a hand and a glimmer of metal. A fan had reached out to me and grabbed a clump of my hair and was just about to cut it off with a pair of scissors. Bob karate-chopped the arm away and I escaped. In trying to block more people from actually gripping on to me to touch me and get some kind of piece of me, Bob had to stretch his arms around me like a dome. As he did this, the buttons on his tuxedo shirt all popped off. He had only the one at the top and the one at the bottom remaining. We eventually got inside the theatre, and Mom used her eyebrow pencil to draw black dots on the button-holes where the buttons would have been. Poor Bob had to suck in his belly as far as he could and maintain perfect posture the entire evening in order not to have his hairy chest exposed. We would eventually laugh at this but it would take me twenty years to even consider returning to the Cannes Film Festival.

The frenzy surrounding *Pretty Baby* in Europe would never be matched in America. Europeans savored the controversy and what they saw as the titillating aura surrounding the film. Most American audiences and critics recognized the film's artistic merits, but they still trashed it. It was called pornography, especially by people who hadn't even seen the film. I was labeled a nymphet whose mother pushed her into inappropriate situations. Canada banned the film. It was fascinating — some of the media were disappointed that I was not more of a Lolita, while others thought the character too provocative and highly inappropriate.

I was shielded from much of the controversy, but I remember being appalled that most people did not see the film's merits. Smart art and film journalists appreciated the film's artistic value, but the controversy meant I had been thrust into a type of cinema purgatory.

I never read any of the reviews of my work, and my mother wanted to keep it that way. If I hinted that I had heard negative comments from the press during interviews, my mom's response was "Fuck 'em if they can't handle it. Are you proud of what you did?"

"Yes."

"Well, then fuck 'em. That's all you need to think about."

Mom kept every single article written about me, my entire life. She had the originals and the duplicates and had them stored in hundreds of banker's boxes. It was not until over twenty years later, as I was writing my first book, *Down Came the Rain,* and cleaning out my storage, that I came upon the enormous collection of reviews. I began reading them and was quickly shocked and immensely hurt. I could not believe the vile way that people wrote about my mother and me. The amount of vitriol directed at us both was devastating. My talent was skewered and my mother's character harshly attacked. I felt relieved that I had not been privy to any of these reviews as a child. I am not sure I would have been able to handle it.

Mom had kept me in a glass case. At first I was content there. It was almost like I was Rapunzel in an enclosed tower, and just as in the fairy tale I was safe, pure, and kept away, at least in my mother's eyes.

Back then, people noticed how naïve I was about everything and found even more to criticize as a result. The press kept asking and speculating about how my mother could allow me to play such provocative parts while keeping me so sheltered. Sometimes even during press events she could be loud or slightly disruptive if she was drinking (which she usually was). And although she was often correct in her judgments on people or situations, she handled almost everything inappropriately. She thought she was the only one in the world who knew better when it came to her daughter. Only she could guide me and give me advice, and anybody who crossed her, in any way, would get written off or not-so-subtly verbally attacked.

In reality, I know Mom was just trying to protect me, but in the long run, she may have gone too far. You can't protect your kids so much that they have no emotional antibodies. She tried to continue to strap me to her chest my entire life. She was undeterred, and as a result many people thought the worst of her. People either decided Mom was the enemy or they appreciated her courage and her ferocity when it came to protecting her daughter.

Thankfully, the negative press did not hinder my chances of working. I did not know how bad and personal the press actually was. I just wanted to keep doing what I was doing. We needed money, of course, and I really loved making movies.

The offers continued to come in, and we now welcomed them all. We began talks with Peter Fonda about a western called *Wanda Nevada*. The movie would take place in Arizona and would star and be directed by Peter Fonda. I played a girl who gets won in a poker game by Peter and travels with him through the Grand Canyon in search of gold. I had to know how to ride horses and be willing to withstand the extreme temperatures of Arizona in August. I told my mom I wanted to do this movie because it was funny and it would be fun living in the Grand Canyon and the remote area of Page, Arizona, that housed the amazing man-made Lake Powell. It sounded like a great way to spend a summer.

We left hot New York City for an even hotter Arizona. We began the trip in a raft on the Colorado River in the Grand Canyon. Because it was summer, I had no teacher or homework. The film schedule was limited because of daylight. We spent more time traveling than we did working. It was like a vacation. There were rides through rapids and campfires and singing and ghost stories. We filmed scenes all along the river, then would pack up, put life vests on, and raft down farther to camp out for the night. We climbed rocks and swam in calm sections and I had a blast. These trips often have steaks and lobsters and other delicacies included in the package. We were feeding a reduced yet still large crew and were traveling with four huge rafts.

At one point, we hit rapids so big that the boat with all the food supplies capsized and we lost all our fancier meals. The raft carrying the craft-service items remained upright, and we were forced to eat peanut butter and jelly, tuna salad, and junk food for the whole trip. Did I mention it felt like a vacation? I didn't mind one bit. Mom was drinking throughout the trip and many of the crew members were smoking weed and doing various drugs, even though I didn't realize the drug part at the time.

I did not mind Mom's drinking as much here in the canyon because we were all so happy and I felt so protected by this close-knit crew. She couldn't really get into any trouble. Morning came before sunrise and bedtime not long after dark. We were all on the same schedule, and even though Mom drank, she seemed happier and kinder to me. I don't remember her being flirty to any crew member or nasty to me at all, so for these ten days, for a change, her drinking was the least important part of the experience.

Every night we all placed our sleeping bags under the stars and settled in. The script supervisor would tickle my back until I fell asleep. Filming in the canyon concluded and we made it to the location for our departure out.

We were met by a pack of twenty or so mules that were to take us out of the canyon and up to the ridge. We loaded up the mules with camera equipment and people and headed out. I was up toward the front of the line near Peter and the cinematographer. It was incredibly exciting, and it was on this movie that I found my real love of moviemaking. It was here that I decided I loved being a gypsy and I loved living different lives and lifestyles.

Unfortunately, my mother had terrible asthma, an affliction I later acquired as well.

While on these mules, inching our way along narrow paths that peered back down into steep canyons, my mother's asthma kicked in. They had placed her somehow at the end of the line of pack animals, and between the mule dander and sweat and the dust being kicked up by mules ahead of her, she had a full-blown asthma attack. In moments, she was unable to breathe and had reached that frightening point when the attack switches from slight tightness in the chest to a debilitating blockage of the airway. She may or may not have had her puffer, but by then it would have been useless. She needed to be airlifted out of the canyon. We stopped and radioed for a helicopter evacuation, and Mom was loaded up and taken to a hospital.

I remember being worried, then embarrassed, then angry. I thought it interesting that it was my mother and not me who created the reason for the upheaval. I knew she did not do it for attention, for as much as she loved being dramatic, Mom did not truly enjoy or feel worthy of the attention. It was designed more to steer people away from her real self. But I remember a flicker of a thought — it seemed like my mother always managed to create a fuss of some sort. Maybe that is why I never did feel the freedom to upset any situation. Deep inside I knew my mom would do it for us. Mom was never too unruly in public if the press was around, but she'd get sloppy. At the birthday bashes she'd throw me, she'd hang on people and dance provocatively. She loved being the wild one and it made me even more reserved.

I was offered a ride on the helicopter to fly out with her, but I chose to remain on my mule. We never spoke about it again and I wonder if she was hurt that I did not choose to go with her. But I wanted to ride out with the team. It was fun and an adventure, and once Mom was safe, I was free to enjoy.

I was always worrying about Mom's safety. I never wanted anything to happen to her and I felt I always had to protect her. When she was asked to leave the Southampton home after pulling the little girl's hair, I thought something bad would happen to her if she were left alone. I would have died for her, as I showed I was willing to do when the Jeep's brakes went out on the George Washington Bridge. In the case with the mule, I relaxed once I knew she was in safe hands.

In a way my refusing the copter ride was one of the first times I chose not to follow my mom anywhere she was headed. This was the first time I can remember choosing myself over her. It is also true that I was able to relax more in this case because I knew my mother was in a professional's care. I knew she wouldn't come to any harm because she was not alone and she was going to be in a hospital. Basically, I found peace in knowing she was accounted for. This was a theme that would run throughout my life and up until the end of hers. As long as I knew my mother was OK, I felt freedom to relax and be present in my life.

Wanda Nevada felt like a camping trip. Because there was nowhere to go but the hotel or the desert, I worried less about my mom. She was drinking as much as always, but I knew where she was and knew she couldn't really get hurt. There wasn't even anywhere to drive, so I felt relaxed. Everybody looked after me and I was, once again, like a mascot. Even my godmother, Lila, who was born in Arizona, was able to meet up with us later in Prescott and stay for a lot of the filming. Mom made no enemies on this set that I can remember. In fact, we made some long-lasting friends. Peter Fonda gave me a chestnut two-year-old filly as a gift and we still speak to this day.

The movie wrapped in mid-September and Mom and I left immediately for Los Angeles. I had been offered a movie with one of my all-time favorite comedians, George Burns.

This movie was called *Just You and Me, Kid* and starred George Burns and a cast of funny and legendary old-time comedians. In the film I play a young runaway who is being chased by the mob. George's character takes me in and we form an unlikely friendship. The movie was shot entirely in Los Angeles and mostly on the Warner Bros. lot. I got my school syllabus and was assigned a tutor; once again Mom's old rule of not missing school had been pushed aside. I loved my tutor, though. She had a great sense of humor and made learning fun. We sent my work back weekly and I continued to do well. In the same way that filming movies gave me refuge from my mom's drinking, time in "school" gave me refuge from shooting. In a very unconventional way, there was a balance to it all. I had no reason to rebel against any of it because each provided a respite from the other and oddly enough gave me a very well-rounded existence.

I was on a roll now and was excited about moviemaking. To me movies represented new, fun, and safe experiences where my mother's drinking would take less of a toll on our lives. There was a safety in having to be responsible to my job and accountable to an outside obligation. It became easier and easier to avoid confronting Mom's drinking and go to a set. I had the excuse of having to work, and it became my ultimate escape. Mom may have been embarrassing or obviously tipsy on set, but there were always other adults, who felt like a sort of extended family, to take me away. They buffered me from my mother's drunkenness and served as witnesses to her behavior. I felt less alone. At home in our apartment I often shrunk from fear and felt isolated. But within the context of moviemaking, there was always somewhere to go and someone with whom to be. Movies felt, at least temporarily, bigger than her addiction. As long as there was a call sheet that outlined the day, I could avoid dealing with Mom's problem for a while longer.

George Burns loved my mom and treated me like a favored grandchild. He refused to light up his famous cigar when around me because he knew I did not like smoking, and we had ongoing inside jokes throughout the filming. Once again, I was treated like a favorite pet.

Filming on an actual movie lot was thrilling to me. The studios looked as if they did in the movies, and it was such a luxury to have a trailer and eat at a commissary or across the street at an old Hollywood restaurant. The SmokeHouse was George's favorite place to eat and he had a regular table. He always invited my mom and me to join him. There he would have fried fish fingers with a side of ketchup and never any alcohol to drink. I always ordered what he had and I wasn't even a fan of fish sticks. I remember Mom ordering her regular drink at the time, which was a martini straight up with a twist, and thinking I was so glad we had only an hour for our lunch break because she wouldn't have time to drink more than about two cocktails.

Mom and I rented a house in Bel Air. It sounds fancy, but it was a run-down ranch-style house with a cracked pool and rats that ate the kiwis we had in a bowl on the kitchen table. I thought it was a mansion and was very excited to live in such a posh neighborhood. Mom and I had fun, and although she was still drinking every night, her days seemed somewhat tempered. If she did drink during the days, I still did not have to get behind the wheel with her because teamsters drove me to and from the set.

It was a happy time. We were working in sunny California and Mom seemed untroubled. My stepsister, Diana, came to stay with my mom and me in our rented house, and, as usual, we all laughed a lot and enjoyed beautiful Malibu and going to Fiorucci or Heaven in Beverly Hills for our Candie's shoes and colored jeans. Looking back now, this seems like it was a bit of a golden era for all of us.

I realize now that I did an incredible amount of work at this time. Five movies in two years! But it made sense for many reasons. I was popular and directors and producers wanted me. But on a personal level, it was just the easiest and happiest way to live with my mother. I still felt incredibly connected to her, but her drinking had become scarier and more difficult.

Mom would not stop drinking for me. I could only believe I wasn't doing enough to make her stop. It took me about thirty years to realize that nothing I did could make her stop if, in fact, she did not want to or could not fight it herself.

But at the time, I still thought I could control things. That I could fix things. And as 1978 ended and I returned to New York, I thought I had finally discovered a way to fix her, this time for good.

CHAPTER SEVEN: ARE YOU FINISHED?

The first thirteen years of my life were unconventional in every way. I lived two entirely different existences between being raised by a single mother and working in the entertainment business and spending time with my father's more conventional (but also more affluent) family. I was a star, but also a normal kid going to regular schools. I was the source of great controversy, yet a darling, an incredibly innocent bystander. The press both praised me and devoured me. Mom was the wild and needy one whereas I was the caretaker and adult. I went in and out of so many different environments and found my comfort zone in all of them. My world was ever changing and diverse, but I had no trouble adapting. Strangely the versatility did not unsettle me but instead fortified me. I grew to know that I could find my place anywhere. At times I did struggle with the question as to who I was because so many others seemed to be living in just one environment and could be defined as such. But I started to have pride in being able to put on a different hat and be a different person, each time learning and loving an undiscovered side of myself.

The circumstances of my daily life were definitely unique, but that was never the reason for my sadness or insecurity. There are clichéd ways of blaming the industry and the press and the public for somebody's demise emotionally, but I cannot ascribe my own troubles to them. I had enough love, good people around me, and a strong-enough innate sense of character to carve a path for myself and admit my own fears or insecurities without placing blame on the world or how unfair things were. I don't know why this was. Even if I had to keep changing directions, I just kept moving. Regretfully, however, I do have to acknowledge that the most damaging element in my life was loving and being loved by an alcoholic mother.

And the problem of my mother's drinking just got worse and worse over the next few months. It's ironic, but I believe that if it were not for the entertainment industry, I would have been a train wreck. I would have crumbled if I did not have a place to hide. I had to be professional because it was my job and I was getting paid. I couldn't fall to pieces.

My dad also provided safety and consistency and a conventional family. I appreciated it and him. I visited often, and even though it felt a bit too restricted and aristocratic at times, the knowledge that his home existed for me came to be a great relief. I found solace in knowing that he was a phone call away. But he was only one part of my life. Most of my time revolved around my mother and what she created.

At work, I was always the good girl, the polite one. I got a good reputation early on because I was so easy to work with. I loved the responsibility because people liking me was the only real reward I sought. The pride I derived from my job stemmed primarily from being liked and accepted. People praised me for being so well-behaved and I was fueled to continue being so.

With regard to my mother, it felt like it was never enough. Nothing I said or did seemed correct or could make her stop getting drunk or feel deeper happiness. I felt helpless. Why wasn't I enough to help her stop drinking? I felt much better about myself when I worked, so I began to crave my jobs. I knew what to expect there. Come the end of my workday, however, I never knew what to expect. It did not seem abusive as much as it did claustrophobic, sad, and helplessly codependent.

In addition, the press wanted me to admit my mother and I had a *Mommie Dearest* type of relationship, but that was simply not the case. She also wasn't Mama Rose, the stereotypical stage mother. I didn't ever have the feeling that she was the one who wanted to be a star. Yes, as a young woman she wanted it all, but with me she was getting it without the risk of falling short herself. She never said, "I could have been . . ." Our relationship and my stardom satisfied all her needs in one. Except she would never feel fully proud of or satisfied with herself. My mother thought she had the most beautiful child in the world. She felt the attention I received was justified. I think she believed in my talent but she never focused on it. She saw people wanting me and that meant success to her. Buying homes and having possessions or traveling meant we were successful.

Looking back at these years I realize that our relationship was so scrutinized because it was so public. But ironically, it was also this public scrutiny that kept me somehow accountable.

I often thought of the private hell that many mothers and daughters were enduring, and I actually felt lucky. I justified my mother's behavior by saying I was lucky I wasn't like the kids out there who were beaten or had relatives who abused them. I just thought my mother was colorful and unconventional. Up until this point, it didn't occur to me that maybe it was unhealthy to live with a mom who drank as much as my mother did and was verbally and emotionally abusive. I believe I also saw how easy it was to focus on people in the public eye when there were so many private sufferers in the world. But I thought that because I was not physically abused or battered, my situation did not merit complaining about or even really fighting.

I knew that although the world thought I was living a crazy life, there were many others whose lives were more tragic. It was this type of empathy that kept me imprisoned by my mother's alcoholism. People assume that if somebody is in the entertainment industry, doom is inevitable. But then I believed those without a public platform were worse off.

The struggles I had never came from the entertainment industry. Stardom, and the fame or money associated with it, was not my issue. The business was my buffer. Stardom was a by-product. It was never the catalyst for my unhappiness. My unhappiness was rooted in my mother's inability to stop drinking. My sense of worthlessness stemmed from feeling insecure as to who I was and inadequate in getting my mother to stop drinking. I had lower self-esteem, not because I was a model but because I was a daughter. The movie business kept me afloat and sane. My mother's drinking superseded my stardom. I was a child of an alcoholic way before I was a star. I craved opportunity and I craved my mother's sobriety. I never understood the connection between the two.

In the end, I never got caught up in my growing fame or my public persona. My focus was always on what was going on at home. My mother's alcoholism tempered the positive and negative ramifications of fame and of being a "star." Between living in New York City, attending nonprofessional children's school, and navigating an alcoholic parent, there was little room for me to fuck up. Fame was easy in comparison. Fame was fake and fickle, but my mom's drinking was real and consistent.

I believed for a long time that I could affect

my mother's drinking. Like many children of alcoholics, I thought if I asked a certain way, or made some type of deal with my mother where I promised something, it would be compelling enough to make her stop.

As I grew older, I started to notice the deeper change in her behavior and began to intensely feel the consequences of the booze. Once, when drunk, she got so angry with me for some little thing that she tipped over a full room-service table. Food went everywhere and one plate bruised the outer part of my eye. I wished it had cut it so I could show her the next day and make her feel bad. Another time we were driving somewhere in the car with Bob and she screamed for him to stop the car. She stumbled out and walked along the highway at night. Bob dropped me off with somebody and spent hours trying to find her. It was especially when I was not working that I felt increasingly unsettled by her drinking.

For years, I didn't know what alcoholism was or that my mother had it. I knew only the effects and I thought I could change them. But at the end of 1978, once we were away from the safety net of the films I had been shooting and back in New York, I was getting scared, both for her and of her. Her drinking seemed to be incessant and her mood swings acute. She had gotten sloppy. I had begged her so many times to quit but to no avail. I knew it was still up to me to do something. I had taken care of her in various ways my entire life and this was just another task.

I think I must have complained to my godmother, Auntie Lila; to Bob; and to my dad. It was probably Lila who introduced me to the concept of alcoholism and how there were people who could help. It is strange how hard it is for me to remember the details and the exact timing, but I distinctly remember walking Mom through the nondescript door of the Freedom Institute, a treatment center in New York that was founded just a few years earlier, in 1976.

It had been only a few weeks prior that I met with a counselor, also at the Freedom Institute, who had described to me what it was to be an alcoholic. She made it clear that Mom had a disease and needed treatment. The counselor explained that I had in no way failed by not being able to get my mother to quit. She clarified that while it was absolutely normal that I wasn't able to get my mother to stop drinking, I was very much needed to help get her into treatment.

This lovely woman exuded kindness and compassion as she took me through the necessary steps in getting my mother help. I listened intently and was resolved to do whatever it took. She kept saying it would be tough and I had to be strong and I was the only one to whom my mother might listen.

I knew I was important because I had been the one navigating my mother's behavior the most intimately and constantly for most of my life. I was the one who had run up the street to Piccolo Mondo in search of Mom and peered in the window at Finnegans Wake pub after school to see if I recognized the back of her head. I was the one who had pleaded with her to not drink on my birthday and made excuses for her when she was on a tear. I was the one who learned that there was no Santa because she was passed out on the couch on Christmas Eve. Of course it would be me who was the important piece in this whole thing.

My mom loved me more than any other human being on the planet. I could fix this — I knew it. Responsibility was a familiar feeling. I absorbed the information and the plan was set. We would stage an intervention and confront my mother. I knew it was a delicate situation and it could go horribly awry. But intervention was my only hope.

I had told my dad that I was going to give my mom an ultimatum. My plan was to tell her I would go live with him and his family if she didn't go into rehab. I remember being aware that I had to present this to my father in such a way that he didn't feel as if living with him was considered a punishment or something I dreaded in any way. I was very sensitive about his feelings as well. But we both knew that the thought of losing me was the only real threat my mother would respond to.

I had been told that in order for intervention to work, it would have to hinge on immediate rehab, because simply getting Mom to promise not to drink, without professional help, had already proven futile. Dad agreed to all parts of the plan; he would wait patiently to hear the intervention's outcome. I can't imagine how he felt hearing his thirteen-year-old child having such resolve.

Finally, the day had come. Auntie Lila had secretly packed a bag for my mother's impending trip. Lila picked me up from school. I somehow got Mom to meet me at the Freedom Institute offices to discuss something serious. It was a nervous, scary time. My mother was never one for surprises, or for any situation, for that matter, in which she did not have complete control. To this day I'm still shocked that she even showed up to meet us.

I remember sitting down with her in a small, poorly lit room. Maybe the lighting was fine or just fluorescent and unflattering, I'm not sure, but I do remember seeing darkness out the sides of my eyes. My vision was narrowing. Lila was there, too. All the sounds in the room, including our voices, had a sort of muffled quality, like we were speaking underwater. I assume now that this was the result of heightened anxiety; I was on the verge of the flight side of the fight-or-flight response.

I did not flee but instead sat down facing my increasingly anxious, soon-to-be-blindsided mother. Once settled, the counselor from the Freedom Institute began giving my mother some background on who she was and what the Freedom Institute was about. She explained that I had come to them some weeks ago to ask for help with my mother's drinking.

I remember immediately thinking that Mom must be getting mad that I went behind her back to discuss her with a stranger. The woman then looked at me and asked me to tell my mother some of the stories I had told her and explain how they made me feel.

I began talking. What could be going through her mind? I imagined Mom saying, "Fuck this," and storming out and going straight to the closest bar. But to my shock, she stayed in her seat. I looked at her and mustered the strength to pretend that I would rather live with my father than with her drinking. For the first time in my life I didn't attempt to get her approval. I kept talking. I explained how mean she got when she drank and how it scared me. I told her I loved her and I wanted to have fun with her but when she drank she changed for the worse.

Her lips pursed and she was silent. One of Mom's go-to tactics in an argument was to keep silent while somebody ranted and then coldly pose the question "Are you finished?" When you said yes, she would basically shut the whole debate down by claiming she would do nothing you asked. How dare you question her?

I expected the same this time. As I spoke about how she acted when she drank and how hurtful she was to me, I had a sort of tunnel vision, the blurry haze that encroaches just before someone is about to faint. Lila chimed in to say that it was mainly for my mother's own benefit that we were doing this. We each had our parts to play. Mom scoffed at the idea of anything *ever* being for her.

The woman from the Freedom Institute said that there had been arrangements made for Mom to go to a place called St. Mary's in Minneapolis, Minnesota. For what seemed like an eternity, there was silence. Then I remember Mom saying she would "think about it."

I thought: *Oh no, we are losing her. I knew it wouldn't work.*

But I didn't give up. We explained that there was actually no time to think it over. That we had her bag ready and that the flight was in a few hours.

Even I felt this was harsh. If it had been me, I would have felt helpless, hurt, and angry. I couldn't tell how she was feeling. My mother's exterior did not betray her emotions, and I could tell she had decided to humor us and play along with this little game we were ignorantly playing, but had not yet decided to concede. She was steely, and I could tell she was upset and hurt and even scared but would never let on.

I knew she was also placating us. She was condescending to our lack of judgment. She was sure she didn't have a problem and would just prove us wrong. She could always turn even the most clear-cut situations into ones where she was calling the shots. She looked only at me and said, "Are you finished?" "Yes, Mama."

More silence and then: She finally spoke. "I'll go. But I am going for *you.* I'm doing this for you, Brookie, *not* for me. I don't have a problem."

She got into the car we had reserved, stoically turned her gaze straight ahead, and that was that. I honestly believe Mom hadn't seen any of it coming.

I didn't understand how I felt as I watched the sedan drive away. I was stunned. At that moment I didn't realize that I would only ever get one chance at such an intervention. I felt relieved Mom had not put up a fight. But I suddenly had the urge to run after the car and apologize and take it all back. I had a pang in my chest and immediately missed her like crazy. I was relieved she was safe. And I was thankful that, in this case, her absence didn't mean she was out at some bar. I instantly felt guilty for having ambushed her and knew she might never forgive me.

The woman from the Freedom Institute sat me down briefly and said we had done well. She said that the important thing was that she had gone. She told me that many people insist they don't have a problem and try to put the burden on the family members and friends doing the intervention. There was a certain pride in the idea that the drinker was taking the high road and doing a loved one a favor by giving in.

Afterward, I remember walking down Third Avenue in a bit of a daze. I felt like it had gone way too easily for total celebration. This should have served as a premonition. Also, with the constant preoccupation of Mom's drinking eliminated, I felt awkwardly unfettered. There would be so much more time to devote to other things; I was suddenly at a slight loss.

Afterward, I went back to our apartment, where Lila would be staying with me for the next few months. I was glad that I didn't have to go live with my father. It wasn't that it would have been terrible, but it would have been inconvenient. I knew it was going to be a hard time. Even being back in the apartment near my mom's things felt suddenly unfamiliar. It felt a bit like a death because we would not even speak to one another for weeks. Phone calls were not allowed.

But life resumed, and Auntie Lila and I

settled in to being roommates. I had a routine at home for the first time, which proved to be a welcome change. I started getting to school on time and eating at the dining table. I admit I loved the feeling of consistency yet felt equally guilty about preferring an ordered way of life compared to the chaos in which my mother lived.

The program lasted three months and included a family week. Auntie Lila and I would visit and engage in group sessions. I remember driving through Minneapolis, seeing big signs for addiction and depression and thinking that Mom had been sent to the right place. Within a day, however, I realized that the dreary place we were visiting was enough to make anybody want to drink. God, it was depressing. I really doubted that this environment would help my mom. But maybe it was supposed to be so bad that people wanted to be clean just so they did not have to return to godforsaken Minneapolis.

It had been a month since I'd seen my mother. During that time we hadn't communicated at all. The separation, the longest we'd ever had by far, felt violent and much like when animals are separated from their mothers for a forced weaning process. However, letters were permitted, and I had sent cards of encouragement. She sent letters back and in one explained how she had already been given the title of group leader and how her counselors continued to praise her. This immediately sent up a red flag to me. My heart sank at the thought that Mom had already seduced the therapy team. She kept alluding to her being the only person at the facility who was different and how, consequently, she was singled out and given more responsibility. I read "superior" as being the underlying subtext. Of course she was running her group. Of course she was not "common." Part of me thought it may have been the truth. Mom had always been unique and set apart from others. I would not learn until years later that this resulted from a sort of self-imposed exile. Mom could not admit to being like the other people in the hospital. They were "crazy" and they had "real problems." My mother's insecurities lay deeply embedded in her psyche. She would prove to be much harder to crack.

Maybe I saw the writing on the wall. Or feared she would outwit the people I had prayed would help. But in any case, I went to family week and resented the whole thing. I hated being there and despised going through the family sessions and lectures.

Luckily, I wasn't quite a household name yet, so anonymity was relatively still on my side. I painstakingly stepped up and did what was asked. Ever the eager front-row, approval-seeking student, I completed the reading material and volunteered in class and spoke about hurt feelings. Yeah, yeah, yeah.

You were encouraged to cry and tell the truth, and for once and for all to come clean. I had already done that. I could not understand why it all had to keep being my problem as well as my mother's. I had done my caretaking and I wanted it to be her turn. When could I be done with it? I was angry that I had to spend my time in dingy Minneapolis, going to lectures on the effects of substance abuse when it was her problem. How could listening to how some redneck father hit his wife help me? Maybe I felt a bit superior as well but the people there were all extremely different from my mother and me. I was miserable, drinking weak coffee with disgusting Cremora. It was nothing like the buttered roll and delicious coffee in Anthora-patterned cups we'd had at home. In this place, I felt like a spoiled little kid who wanted to stamp my feet and storm out of the room.

I couldn't identify with any of these

people or their stories. I had been told that I would meet people much like me in this environment and finally feel supported and fortified. It could not have been further from the truth. I could not have felt more isolated. I don't mean that the differences stemmed from the fact that I was a "movie star." The truth was that there was a cultural difference with regard to references and complaints. The people were actually lovely but I felt I was in a foreign country. The problem was that Mom was indeed savvier than many of the people at the facility; I could only imagine my mom reprogramming and manipulating each one of them. I had been told that once I realized that others had gone through the same experience I had by living with an alcoholic, I wouldn't feel so alone, but in this case, the booze seemed to be the only underlying similarity.

I honestly didn't fit in there, and I worried that Mom actually did not, either. Mom was one of those unbelievably sly, influential drunks who could hook you in, all the while cutting you down. It was borderline sociopathic, minus the murder. St. Mary's was, and is, a great and reputable institution that came highly recommended and regarded, but sadly it was not a good or effective fit for my mother. Had I made a mistake? Was Mom right, once again? I felt Mom really was smarter than most of the patients and even cleverer than some of the counselors. Why had I not been even smarter than she was for once? She was right again! Mom wasn't, however, smart enough to choose health over addiction. I wouldn't realize until many years later that my doubts were all part of my codependence. The venue may or may not have been ideal for her, but it was not necessarily because she was too much of a genius. It was more a product of her inability to be honest with herself or strong enough to choose to be healthy.

Aunt Lila and I completed our "family week" and left Mom to finish out her stay. Mom made one lifelong friend at St. Mary's. Except for one relapse a few years later, Mom's friend would remain sober for the rest of her life. I always wished Mom had been that type of a recovering alcoholic.

Overall, Mom played by the rules but never did the "steps." I don't believe she ever committed authentically, and the therapy never fully registered with her. She used the recovery catchphrases like a dutiful student. But all the while she was scoffing at how they didn't actually apply to her. She beguiled the staff with her humor and her street smarts. She was incredibly intuitive about the way others behaved and what their needs were. She could outwit almost anyone. But, sadly, she was still an alcoholic and hardly two steps closer to recovery.

I truly believe she thought she didn't have a problem and that she could control her drinking. But I'm not convinced she ever did the work that would help her get there. Vulnerability equaled weakness for my mom. One of the early steps in AA deals with admitting helplessness about your problem. Well, being helpless was never something Teri Terrific could cop to. I don't believe she ever fully admitted to the severity and authenticity of her disease.

Mom returned home after three months. I made a sign and got her flowers to celebrate her homecoming. Lila and I had taken a photo of us together and had put it in a little frame. It was the kind you get in a photo booth. Mom for some reason got so angry that it was of the two of us that she tore it up. I told her it was only supposed to mean we loved her. Shockingly that was where my sweetness ended. In the next few weeks and months I was horrible to her in any way that I could be. I may have been lashing out and punishing her for years of drinking. I may have been testing her to see if she would crack and start drinking again. Maybe I was just so uncomfortable with her sobriety that I was acting out.

I was putting her on trial for some reason, and I got a quietly maniacal thrill when I hurt her. I felt terrible about it, but in a weird way, I wanted to create a new dysfunction because that is what was familiar.

I couldn't stop being nasty to her. Yet she neither fought me nor began drinking just yet. It was all so awkward and foreign, and I realized I had no idea how to act around her when she was sober. I was so used to navigating her drinking and being sad, angry, or afraid, that without the existence of trauma, I was floundering. I hated her drinking but at least I knew what to expect. The protocol of being the child of an alcoholic was second nature to me, so without it I was again slightly lost.

I also realize that, in a way, I saw myself as a better person than she was when she drank. I liked that feeling. Most of my life I just wanted my mother's approval. But admittedly, when she was drunk, there was a type of freedom for me. I was justified in fighting her when she drank, but take away the booze and I just didn't know what to fight.

I could have never anticipated it, but I unexpectedly hated her for her sobriety. If Mom and I were not getting along for some reason or if I was feeling the growing pains that all kids go through, I did not have anything on which to place blame. It was very unsettling facing her insecurities and her behavior without accusing the booze. Having the troubles actually be a part of my mother's deeper personality was even more tragic. I even secretly wanted her to start drinking again so I could say, "I told you so. I knew you couldn't do it."

I was also so angry at St. Mary's and the Freedom Institute for seemingly having more control over my mommy than I did. It was all so fucked-up and confusing and I began lashing out at everybody.

The sweeter she was, the more I punished her. The more people tried to help me, the more I stomped and pouted. I even turned against Lila and cast her aside emotionally. On top of all that, I was getting my period for the first time and my hormones made me an emotional and irrational mess. I had been used to my codependence, and as much as I thought I wanted it, I was resisting the change. I wanted to hurt my mother. It was plain and simple. I pushed and pushed until I got tired.

■ ■ ■ ■

I don't know how she did it, but my mother didn't crack. She stayed steady and loving. She was the most mature I had ever seen her. Maybe they'd told her at St. Mary's to expect difficult behaviors from family members. But for whatever reason, she waited it out, but it remained.

There was no alcohol to blame or to retreat toward. We all needed to adjust to this new dynamic.

The tragic part to me now is how idealized I had made her recovery. As a child of an alcoholic, I believed in a silver lining. One day it would all be better. I believed in the idea of a promise. Once this or that milestone was reached, then she would see and she could smile. One day she would be happy.

But the truth was that as kind as she was being, Mom had trouble being honest with herself about anything. How could she suddenly morph into this fully resolved and self-actualized being? I don't think my mother ever released her pain or her hurt, and therefore her healing was going to require more than just stopping drinking. I could not know this then. I was just baffled at how there was no rainbow.

I don't remember ever being told at the time what I learned later, which is that even if you remove the alcohol, there is still unresolved pain and hurt in a relationship. Damage has often been inflicted by both the drinker and those closest to the drinker. It must be acknowledged.

But just because the booze went away, it didn't mean the damage went with it. The term *dry drunk* means that the drinking may not be current but the precipitating feelings that drive the drinker to abuse alcohol have not gone away. People told me that drinking revealed a person's true personality, but I could never believe that. I refused to believe that, deep down, my mom was honestly that ugly. I did believe that deep down she could have been that damaged and hurt, but not ugly. There were wounds that needed to be faced and attended to for both of us. The problem was, however, that for me, I didn't want to ruin these moments of sobriety by stirring up my old hurts. It is so much easier to sweep them all under the carpet and pretend they never existed. This, unfortunately, took a toll.

My mother really did seem to try to stay sober at first. I could tell it was tough for her. I even dreamed of a world in which she could be able to drink moderately. Addicts must abstain completely. There is no such thing as an alcoholic being able to be a social drinker, but I secretly wished that she could find a way to reasonably drink so we could all be happy. This is how codependent my thoughts were and how much I wanted her to enjoy life and be healthy and happy. Because if she was happy, I did not have to worry. I never liked any part of her when she was drinking. She may have been fun for others but I really authentically enjoyed her only before she took her first sip. When she laughed sober, I felt oxygen in my blood.

I really thought everything would be better if she stopped drinking. But it wasn't. We fell back in the same patterns, just with different details. It was time to do something new and different. To go far away and get back to the golden age and good feelings we'd had shooting movies in the past and sticking my head in the sand about everything else. And as luck would have it, my next movie role would take us farther away than I could have imagined.

CHAPTER EIGHT:
BLUE

In early 1979, just as my mother and I were adjusting to post-rehab life, I got an intriguing offer. An author named Henry De Vere Stacpoole wrote a novel back in 1908, *The Blue Lagoon,* that had already been made into a movie twice. The first version was from 1923. It was black-and-white, silent, and filmed in England. Neither my mother nor I knew anything about the silent version, but my mother was a fan of the 1949 version, which was filmed in both England and Fiji and starred Jean Simmons and Donald Houston. Mom had loved Jean Simmons and thought the idea of a remake was wonderful.

The Blue Lagoon tells the story of two cousins, Emmeline and Richard Lestrange, who survive a shipwreck and grow up together on a tropical island in the South Pacific. Through most of the movie they're completely alone, eventually developing a romantic relationship and having a child.

Shooting this film meant we'd be on location again, this time for months. We'd leave for the South Pacific in June and not return until September. Mom and I had always loved being on location. It was like this great sanctuary in which I worked hard and Mom played hard. We were excited and I was anticipating feeling relieved because Mom had not been drinking and I believed her sobriety would continue on this deserted island. After all, there would be no bars.

The director, Randal Kleiser, who had just had a huge success directing the movie *Grease,* and the studio, Columbia Pictures, wanted Matt Dillon to play my character's cousin, a choice that thrilled me. But Matt's mother was against the idea and they turned it down. I was devastated because I knew Matt and thought he was cute and talented. He was very sweet about the whole thing and made it a point to tell me that his decision was in no way a personal affront to me.

The filmmakers began to search for someone to play Richard. This choice was, obviously, a very big deal for me, since the two of us would basically be the only actors in the entire movie. Minus some flashbacks it would be just us. By this time I had been in seven films and was very worried about working with an amateur. The studio finally found a kid with straight blond hair and a beautiful physique who had no film or acting experience and had spent his extracurricular time as an athlete. The director had called to tell us that they had found my counterpart, an eighteen-year-old student from Rye, New York, whose dream had been to go into sports medicine. His name was Christopher Atkins and I was going to love him! I was skeptical but had no say and his photo looked fine. I had worked with many veterans but this would be the first time that I was the actual veteran.

Mom and I packed our suitcases, sent our two rescue cats to a boarding house, and left for the island of Vanua Levu in Fiji. We had to fly to the mainland and to the city of Lautoka, via Australia, and then take a seaplane to Turtle Island, where we would be living for the next four months.

We touched down on water and taxied to the dock, where were met by Randal and Chris and some Fijian men to help with the bags. Chris's light-blond, naturally stick-straight hair had been given a perm. I didn't understand why it was necessary for him to have curly hair but it was not up to me to decide. He looked different from his photo but cute. Once on the dock, I was instructed to leave my bags to be taken to where we would be staying and go directly to the tanning area. Some preparations needed to start right away. There was still enough sunlight to get color and I was told I needed to start to build up enough of a tan so that it looked as if I had been living on an island my entire life. The tanning space consisted of two small areas enclosed by mats of woven palm fronds. I was to take off all my clothes and begin that day by getting a base. Chris had already been on the island for a week so he was already darker than I was. I would have to catch up. I was told I could choose to live on the big sailing ship that would be featured in the film or I could remain on land.

At first, I was sure I'd choose the ship. I had this fantasy that I would have a quaint little cabin where I would write in my journal and be rocked to sleep nightly. I would stick pictures on my wall and write letters to my friends back home and it would be as if I was part of an expedition a hundred years ago. But after getting off the scary seaplane that sat only three people and being confronted with the real-life version of my fantasies, I took one look at the ship and changed my mind. It was ancient and had rats and creaking planks. I opted for a *bure,* or hut, as non-Fijians called them.

The bure I would share with my mother was right on the beach and basically consisted of a cinder-block square with a standing sink and a partitioned-off toilet.

The rafters were big palm-tree trunks and the roof was a thatched canopy with a peak. The shape of the roof enabled rain to cascade down the sides and not leak into the room. Our bure consisted of two connecting rooms, each with two twin beds. This was perfect for when I had friends visit from the States.

The first few weeks we rehearsed and prepared to film, and Chris couldn't have been sweeter. He was so excited, energetic, and kind all the time and took me on tours of all the special spots in our new home away from home.

He was really cute and I think everybody was even secretly hoping that we would become a real-life couple. I could tell that Randal, the director, really wanted it, and he enlisted my mother to be encouraging as well. Even though it was not overt, I felt people believed it would be good for the film. God forbid we just act! Chris seemed equally excited to become my best friend and possible boyfriend and was always around me. Anyway, if it was going to happen anywhere, this stunning island would be the perfect environment in which to fall in love. I, however, began to feel standoffish. I have never been good with people forcing themselves on me, or acting too gung-ho about becoming my closest buddy. The moment I sensed the push, I put up a wall so tall that my mother had to tell me to give the kid a break and not take it out on him. I would have none of it and their plan almost backfired. But he really was so sweet and happy that I would eventually develop a crush on him. It lasted only a very short time because Chris and I were really more like brother and sister than we were lovers. Strange that our relationship was actually closer to the essence of the film than even others could see.

Mom explained that Chris probably believed he had to fall in love with me to be a good actor. I was going to teach him otherwise. Even though Chris originally came across a bit strong and off-puttingly eager, I really did respect how he was committing to his debut role. Chris had learned to spear fish, skin-dive, build a thatched hut, and start a fire with sticks. He was trying to be as authentic as he could and I appreciated his approach. I, too, committed to learning whatever I could from the locals.

Like Chris, I set out to adapt immediately. Within two weeks I could climb palm trees in bare feet, dive for coral and shells without a tank and without making bubbles, and weave palm fronds into bowls and small boxes for catching rainwater. I had worked up to holding my breath for over a minute so I could do the underwater scenes more efficiently. I jumped right into being an island kid, rarely wearing shoes, and swimming whenever I could. Mom and I both chose to tie traditional *sulus* around ourselves instead of wearing shorts and T-shirts. A sulu is almost exactly like an Indian sari or a wrap you often wear at the beach. They are made of brightly colored cotton and can be tied many different ways.

We learned the difference between eating coconuts right off the tree and those that had fallen on the ground. One Fijian man in particular taught me to use a pointed stick and a machete to break open mature coconuts for their meat and young ones for their milk. Our crew consisted mostly of Australians and Americans, but included a few sturdy Fijians. The native Fijians spoke very little English, but with the few words they did know, and with the Fijian I picked up, we communicated fine.

I forget his name but the man who taught me about coconuts was the same man who made my mother a long sword from wood so she could beat away the rats that moved into our roof. The rats had moved in a few weeks after Mom and I began living there. They were really terrible and seemed to come out mostly late at night. I hated rats and slept with the blankets over my head. I pictured them landing on my head in the middle of the night and chewing my face off. I'd hear Mom leap up and start whacking at the thatched-roof ceiling after hearing a scurry. I don't think my mother ever slept.

We all got used to living on a deserted island and dealing with everything that came along with it, such as rats, bugs, sewage issues, mail once a week, storms, and sunburn. Only one man had ever lived on this island with his wife. He owned it, and his dream had been to eventually turn it into a resort.

The cinematographer, Academy Award winner Néstor Almendros, used only natural light and fire to light the entire film. In order to complete a day's worth of scenes, we needed as many hours as possible, so Néstor came up with the idea of pushing our clocks ahead. Everyone working on the film synchronized his or her watch to a new time. Each morning I had to get up at 5:00 A.M. or even earlier. So while my clock said 5:00 A.M., for my body it was actually 4:00 A.M. Mom was never a good sleeper and rarely slept more than five hours a night, sober or not. But the benefit of this self-imposed time shift, which we dubbed Bula Time, was that except for all-night shooting, which was lit by fire and candlelight, we would finish our days by dusk. Sometimes, immediately after filming for the day, Chris and I would go diving for shells. I was collecting white shells that had rays of red dots that fanned to the tip. It took me weeks, but I collected enough of them to make my mother a necklace for her birthday. Sometimes, if I was lucky, I'd find a piece of black coral and string it on to some leather for myself.

My skin had trouble holding on to a tan and I began losing all pigmentation. Patches of white began appearing, so to avoid looking like I was starring in *The Jungle Book* as a leopard instead of in a love story about sun-kissed teenagers, I had to get up even earlier than everyone else so I could be sponge-painted with makeup mixed with iodine. The makeup lady used big natural sea sponges and spread the liquid all over my body until I was the desired color. I was only allowed to take limited showers, and then only on days when we had finished a sequence the day before. The feeling of being painted by wet, cold sponges before dawn every morning was, to this day, one of the worst feelings I have ever experienced.

Our one day off a week was Sunday. Mom and I were getting along much better these days. My rage toward her had subsided and we were back in a routine we loved. Mom and I both loved to create new little lives for ourselves. Wherever we went, we would make it a home. We decorated our huts and wore traditional attire and played the music of the Fijian people. But we maintained some of our own traditions. Mom and I would wake up early and take a small motorboat to a mission on a neighboring island. It took forty-five minutes and we wore no life vests. For much of the trip no land was visible. Then, off in the distance, I'd see the outline of the small island and the steeple of a church. Mom and I attended Catholic Mass every Sunday with the nuns from the mission, who also taught the children their lessons. I kind of dreaded the idea of having to trek so far to go to church, but I loved being on the open water so early in the morning, and the service was always sweet and filled with singing.

One of our Fijian crew members enjoyed the ride and would come with us to do the navigating. At the conclusion of the shoot, my mother arranged for the film company to donate our generator to the mission. This generator enabled them to have electricity for the first time in their lives. The nuns loved my mother, who made them laugh and donated much of my per diem to them weekly. They needed it more. There was nothing else to spend the small weekly amount provided by the producers on, so it was no loss to me. My long hair fascinated the schoolchildren and it took me a while to get used to them wanting to touch it. I often had to remind myself I was not in Cannes.

We would return to our island in time to have a big breakfast or take a nap. Many Sundays and most nights, while walking back to my bure, I'd pass the local men having their nightly kava ceremony. Kava is a root that when crushed and placed inside a man's tube sock, and then soaked in water, makes a liquid resembling dirty dishwater that tastes like mud. It is served in half a coconut shell and if offered cannot be refused. It was considered rude, and unlucky, to refuse the call of "Kava, kava, *bula* kava!" Whenever I passed the ceremony, I'd try to go unnoticed, but I often failed and was forced to accept a cup. You were supposed to swallow the liquid from your coconut in one gulp. After ingesting this disgusting, lukewarm substance, you had to clap three loud, hollow-sounding claps with cupped palms, before passing it on to the next willing victim. I never learned what the claps symbolized but it was part of the ceremony. Kava numbs your mouth and throat and gives you a sedated feeling. The effects did not last too long, especially if you drank only one cup, but the taste was so disgusting and I hated it so much that I tried to avoid the torture whenever possible. Mom never got into it, either, because she said she didn't like the feeling. I was surprised they offered it to a kid, and I did not find it fun or cool.

It wasn't long before Mom began drinking again. The moment I saw the look on her face I knew. She got the usual flushed cheeks and familiar blurry eyes, and of course her lips had their signature brittle-looking texture. I always asked her to breathe out so I could smell her breath, and she'd come very close and open her mouth but never exhale. She despised the idea of my trying to control her in any way. I made it clear that I was aware that she had started up again. She had halfheartedly tried to conceal it from me, and then before long, it was every night, out in the open, and with zero remorse. I believe Mom simply felt drinking was her prerogative. If she wanted to get drunk, then she would get drunk, and as long as I was OK or fit her definition of *cared for,* then she saw no downside.

What I felt were the personal consequences of her drinking, consequences that she saw as insignificant. If I got hurt because she said I could be a "bitch" or in a rage that she hated me, she'd dismiss my feelings. Because she knew she loved me, and because she knew I believed she loved me, none of it mattered. She had no idea how deeply her mean comments, whether representing her true feelings or not, cut into my heart.

I was devastated at Mom's inability to stick to the program and her failure to stay clean. I felt angry that she did not keep her promise. Mom, however, never seemed ashamed by her choices — choices that I clearly regarded as displays of weakness. She would never issue forth any apology or justification. She just did what she wanted to do. I'd yell at her when she was drunk and told her I hated her, but she knew I loved her so she let the insults roll off her like water. I never talked to her sober about any of it. Why ruin the moment? We avoided all of it and all the rules of recovery, and I never expressed how deeply pathetic I thought it was that she could not control herself. But I had learned that accusing my mother of being even remotely inept in any way could easily result in disaster. She held a power over me. I mostly kept my mouth shut and instead pouted around her, hoping to give off an air of disappointment.

I felt like I lost my mother every time she drank. I felt completely alone and on edge all the time waiting to see if she had been drinking or was about to drink. I was always afraid of what she'd say when drinking. I was embarrassed by her cursing and flirting with crew members and was grossed out by everything about her attitude and appearance. I lived inside my stress and in a constant state of anticipation of the possible wreckage of the future.

Here, however, I wasn't concerned about her safety. There was nowhere my mother, nor anybody, could really disappear to on this island, so some of my fears dissipated. Unless she went swimming, the risks were fewer here than in a city. Mom didn't even know how to swim, so there was no worry of her going for a midnight dip and drowning. I guess she could have been trampled by the wild horses that roamed the island, or been nibbled on by the rats or the huge stone crabs that had invaded our camp, but this did not concern me. Soon, however, I began to compartmentalize, as I had learned to do years back. I just gave up emotionally. I hated her drinking, but I could not seem to do anything about it, so I buried my head and my anger in the proverbial (and fitting term for island living) sand. Once again, because I was on a movie set, and there was work to do and other people around, this was quite easy to do.

There was a real safety in being on an

island that was seven miles long and a mile wide, with no roads or potential vehicle accidents. All this comforted me, but it especially helped that I had my favorite student-teacher and social worker on location with me, and I felt protected watched over by her. Her name was Polly and I requested her every time I got a job. She had been with me on many jobs and I adored being with her. We had the same sense of humor and had an incredible amount of fun together.

Mom must have felt confident knowing that Polly was watching over me, and was emboldened to drink even more. Often, at night, Mom would stay behind in the makeshift bar the crew had put together, and Polly would bring me back to our bure at bedtime. For this movie Polly acted as more of a companion and a caretaker than a teacher because it was summer vacation. She really kept an eye on me, occupied my time — which helped me not obsess about Mom's drinking — and even made sure the director did not try to talk me into doing my own nude scenes behind my mother's back.

Mom had insisted on a body double, and everybody was made aware of this fact. For the full-nudity scenes I would have a double, but for the seminude ones I would be somehow covered. I wore an extremely long wig, made from real hair, and it was long enough to cover my breasts. Even though my boobs were nonexistent, by the age of fifteen I had become self-conscious. The hair was long enough to cover them, but because of the wind, we had to secure the pieces to my skin with toupee tape. I called it tuppy tape, and every day when I took it off I'd stretch each strip as far as it would go. Toupee tape has a fun elasticity, and this activity became a tradition, bordering on an OCD tick for me. I'd have to stretch every strip or I got superstitious. I developed various mini-habits or neatening actions over the years and realize now that they were reactions to the frustrations and helplessness I felt toward Mom's drinking.

After all the controversy surrounding *Pretty Baby,* I am sure that Mom was even more adamant about not having her daughter be nude. Mom loved reiterating this fact to the press. Even though the producers hated the press knowing I had a double, because they said it threatened the integrity of the film, Mom loved telling the world. She felt it proved to people that she had my best interests at heart. I always found it fascinating that a Hollywood producer's idea of "protecting the integrity of a film" involved having a minor do her own nude scenes.

The company had trouble finding a suitable body double, so they ended up using thirty-year-old diver Valerie Taylor, who, with her husband, Ron, was responsible for filming the underwater shots. The couple had filmed all the water scenes for the movie *The Day of the Dolphin* and could hold their breath calmly and for minutes at a time. The first time Valerie dove into the water wearing my long, natural wig, the hair almost instantly matted up in a big mess. She came out of the water with a matted clump of hair worthy of Rastafarian status, and the shot had to be postponed. The wig, which came from England, was quite thick and cost thousands of dollars, and we had only one. Until we found another identical wig from England, we couldn't film any of my scenes. They ended up having to get a synthetic wig for all the underwater shots. Mom loved highlighting how ignorant these people were not to know a natural-hair wig should not get soaked.

As filming continued, Chris and I went through a myriad of phases in our friendship. It began with my resenting the pressure I felt from the director to actually fall in love; then we actually had short crushes on each other; then he annoyed me and I'd not talk to him for a while except on film; then we'd forget all about the fight and act like friends again. Maybe it was love! We were more like siblings, and midway through the filming I remember Chris even moving into our bure.

Mom insinuated that she saw something she thought inappropriate, and thought it best if he stayed closer to us because nobody would mess with him if she were around.

Then I had to face the relationship between the director and *his* tanned, blond boy. I am not saying it was romantic, but the director was seemingly infatuated. The boy was, of course, Chris, and it made me crazy. I was less jealous than I was frustrated by how obviously enamored the director was with this Adonis. I felt constantly disregarded. No matter what I did, or what my mom said to me to make her feel better, I hated it. The attention remained on Chris. Chris would be doing a take and the director would marvel at how extraordinary his talent was.

He'd say, "You, Brooke, you're the pro, but look at him; he's a natural!"

I could feel my jaw clenching and the

jealousy mounting. I'd complain to my mom, saying he was a rookie and thought he knew everything and the director just played into this behavior. She'd tell me to forget it, adding that the director was probably in love with the kid. Mom often made quick judgments about things like this. She would often say somebody was probably jealous of me or that that director "had a thing for" that actor or actress. She wanted to be the one who saw everything and knew everything. She was confident that I would believe her wholeheartedly.

At one point the tension got so bad for me that I began disliking how Chris even held his hands. I became competitive with him. I wanted the director to approve of my work as much if not more than he approved of Chris's. It was obvious that I was not going to succeed in this way. I found little ways to bug him and prove I was better than he was. I'd follow him around on set and sing the lyrics to Supertramp's "Take the Long Way Home."

"So you think you're a Romeo, playin' a part in a picture show. . . ."

While filming water scenes, I tried to hold my breath longer underwater than he did and find more black coral than he did. I declared that I could drink more kava than he could and crack open a coconut faster. Truth be told, though, he could swim better and climb coconut trees faster than I could. I memorized my lines faster and I would correct him on his own if he messed up. I was basically being a brat. It never got ugly, thank God, and, over time, I got over needing constant approval from the director. Our angel cinematographer also noticed my needs and chose specific and necessary times to praise me.

Chris and I were never romantic, and because most of the intimate scenes in the film were between Chris and my body double, our relationship stayed platonic. They had to be nude together, but all I had to do was kiss him a few times.

I find it interesting that, once again, I was able to uphold a certain sense of innocence in what had been considered a provocative environment. My mom was with me on the island, but I was older than I was in *Pretty Baby* and I was rather self-assured. People really loved my mother on this movie. She was not viewed as a threat as if she had been by Polly Platt, and we were in a very contained space. She may have unsettled Randal by her mere attitude and proximity, but for the most part they all got along. There was a raw quality to this movie. We were all isolated together and in it for the long haul. It was safe and we were all connected and we were a team. Because people genuinely embraced her, I think she put up fewer defenses. There was something about the Aussies. They just knew how to meet people where they were, without judgment but with humor and a sense of adventure. Because they overlooked Mom's deeper insecurities, they were a perfect group for both of us.

Plus, the Aussies knew how to party, so my mom fit right in. Even on this location, Mom was able to find ways to keep busy.

She'd often try to make calls to the mainland or help organize parties and themed events for the cast and crew.

God knows Mom loved a party and enjoyed being a part of any event where drinking was practically a prerequisite. A few times she took a seaplane to the mainland and delivered mail or brought back film, magazines, and even pizzas. Although the pizza delivery came to a quick halt when we turned over a slice only to find rat droppings embedded in the dough!

By this time Mom was drinking as if she had never stopped. It was like it had all been a dream. It was such a shame, but there was so much alcohol at base camp and around this crew that it was evidently just irresistible to her. Excessive consumption was not out of the norm for this lot, and it was very accepted. It's amazing I never started then. I hated that Mom got drunk with the crew as much as she did, and I could not believe that after all the angst we went through for her treatment, it felt as if nothing had changed. Mom had started back up again as easily as she had gotten into that car on the curb waiting to take her to the airport to go to a facility. I tried to just remove myself emotionally and, when I could, physically.

But by the end of August, I had hit a limit with island life. As much as I had submersed myself in that sandy oasis, I was ready to go home. Mom was equally ready to leave. She never went in the sun and I don't remember her ever even going in the water. We were both ready for some of the tastes and comforts of home. We had become an incredibly tight-knit team, who experienced and suffered a great deal with one another, but I was homesick for New York. Shooting this movie had had an impact on all of us based purely on the long hours and sometimes intensely tough weather and living conditions, and we were all exhausted. We had lived through sicknesses, injuries, breakups, and even deaths of loved ones during filming. I still have scars lining my Achilles tendon from cuts that had ulcerated from swimming in water near a coral reef. It had been an intense, wonderful, and sometimes surreal experience, but it eventually got to all of us. Being away from home and from modern conveniences took its own toll, and we all needed an extended break from the island and from each other.

The first time I actually wrapped production, we were all packed and had taken off for and landed on the mainland of Suva. Mom and I went to a hotel to rest and wait the five hours necessary before catching our flight back to the States. After about an hour, we were contacted at the hotel and informed that some of the film had been damaged, and I was needed for an additional two weeks of filming. My heart sank. I cried when I realized I had to wait two more weeks before returning home. Cutting my hair all off would have had no impact on this movie because I wore a wig, so I felt even more helpless.

I'll never forget the real last day, when we were finally able to leave. We were doing one last scene on the beach. Before it was over, the seaplane arrived. It coasted to the dock and waited. I remember looking at it and thinking that no matter what happens, the moment I start walking on that dock, I am not stopping. I told Mom I didn't care if the film blew up; I was going home. She concurred.

There was a part of me that also did not ever want to leave Nanuya Levu. Not because it had been paradise, but because on this island it felt easier to keep my mother alive. Losing Mom was a constant fear of mine, but these four months the panic surrounding her possible death had waned slightly.

We took off for the mainland, and as I saw our island getting smaller and smaller, my mind wandered to the impending future of my mom's drinking. Dread began creeping back into my stomach. Without the containment of the island and the protection of the crew, I would be alone with her alcoholism yet again. Mom and I had been in somewhat of an unrealistic bubble in the middle of nowhere, but once back in New York City she would be on the loose again. I would no longer easily know her whereabouts. The island and the crew and the tough schedule had provided me with a huge safety net, but now that this protective zone was receding, my heart began to grow heavy. Before long, I would be resuming my hypervigilance.

Intervention and rehab had been a mere apparition. I was going back to square one in the battle to survive my mother's disease.

We got to the mainland and would have to wait for the 2:00 A.M. connecting flight. We would have dinner at the hotel plus a few hours of rest. Then we'd fly back to the United States and it would begin to feel like it had all been a dream.

The Blue Lagoon had a huge premiere a year later, in June 1980, at the famous Cinerama Dome in Los Angeles. It was my first time at this theatre and it was quite exciting. The building seemed immense and I was blinded with light and by the sight of Chris's and my face covering the entire side of the building. There was excitement and anticipation in the air. My stepsister, Diana, came out to be with me for the press junket and kept me laughing the entire time. This was something that Mom had negotiated into my contract. This was unprecedented — getting the studio to pay for a companion for me during a junket. But it kept me contented, so they couldn't fight it. It was good for everyone.

Mom even had a friend flown in to the island to visit. I'm not sure if the studio paid for the ticket but she always negotiated multiple tickets so I could have a friend or Diana come to visit. Mom felt it important for me not to feel lonely or stressed by the press, who as we knew could be unkind. I needed a partner in crime. This was an unheard-of request, but I had no agents or publicists for the studio to pay for, so Mom could justify the expense. According to her, they were getting off easy. My mother and Diana were my entire entourage. Diana understood Mom's battle with booze and she also loved and laughed with my mom. She was on our side.

I was so happy to have Diana there. Press junkets are pure torture. You go to a hotel and whole floors are invaded and occupied by different press outlets. The actors and director trade off from room to room and do back-to-back interviews of about five to seven minutes each. You could do forty-two interviews before lunch. It's mind-numbing because of the repetition. I kept getting questions like "What was it like living on an island?" and "Were you and Chris Atkins really in love?" and "Did you do your own nudity?"

I could answer these questions in my sleep. In fact, Mom, Diana, and I had a running joke about how a journalist would not even have to ask one question and I could give them a complete interview. After surviving *Pretty Baby*'s press tour, I was a pro on nudity and romance and the rigor of filmmaking.

It got to the point that I started answering the questions before the journalist even finished the question. Finally my mom, who would watch my interviews, took me aside and reminded me to allow the interviewer to get the question out. We had a big laugh about that. On our lunch break in the hotel room, I posed as a journalist and Diana pretended to be me answering the questions. We thought it was hysterical. Chris played along, and he and Randal did their own version. We made an otherwise tedious necessity fun and silly.

We kept things interesting in other ways. Randal would quietly sing the words to the Robbie Dupree song "Steal Away" under his breath as we passed in the hallways on the way to the next "firing squad," as I nicknamed the press. We were all so bored and tired and all wished we could just run out the door and escape. Having the spurts of laughter and my stepsister and mother doing whatever they could to keep me laughing made it all more enjoyable and helped me maintain perspective. I was also excited because Mom promised that once I had finished my obligations, I could go shopping. Mom would let me loose in the store and Diana and I would spend all my per diem. The combination of this, good restaurants, and hanging out wearing our hotel robes was enough to sustain me.

All I kept thinking during these press days was that the journalists were all going to slaughter me in this movie. It just seemed to me that after *Pretty Baby,* it was decided that I was worthy of attack. Mom would not be able to shield me as entirely as she had from the negativity of *Pretty Baby,* but at least that had been a European director and an incredible cast.

This was a cast of two, and I carried most of the burden of ensuring its success. I suppose I was more equipped to handle it by then, but I was slightly apprehensive. I knew enough by this point to be concerned but realized there was nothing I could do.

The movie made a huge splash and was a box-office hit, ultimately the ninth-highest-grossing film of 1980. The studio was over the moon, and I was once again a commodity they coveted. But strangely, I never paid much attention to how my movies did. In my mind, they were done, and I was thinking about my next job. If I had enjoyed making the movie, then it was a success in my eyes.

I'm also glad that I was unaware of the true power of ticket sales. I didn't pore over the reviews this time, either, and because I sort of couldn't be bothered, I remained somewhat protected from any negativity. There were mixed reviews for *The Blue Lagoon,* and Mom did not hide them from me as actively as she had with *Pretty Baby.* I also didn't really ask to read them. I simply wanted to move on. I had done the movie and it was over. A year had passed. I was attending a new school and had basically moved past the experience. Plus, I did not want to hear bad critiques; I knew they would attack me and I knew my feelings would get hurt. For whatever reason, I subconsciously knew that it was probably healthier for me to be somewhat separated from the reviews.

Thinking about it now, though, I am a bit conflicted about the fact that I did not read reviews. Perhaps if I had read the reviews, I may have chosen to steer my career differently. Perhaps I could have made better choices or might have given it all up entirely. I will never know.

Once the press junket was over and we were back in New York for good, Mom and

I fell into our familiar pattern. We kept busy: I studied, she drank, we went to the movies, she drank, I navigated her moods, and she drank.

I had hoped that a fresh start and a successful film would make everything easier. But the more in demand I became, the more complicated everything got. My mother reacted to the press by defending herself to journalists like Barbara Walters or by choosing to give random interviews to the press. Normally you don't see the talent's manager on TV, but she was my mom and the world ate it up. She wanted to prove she was still protecting me and that she was guiding my career in the best way possible. She loved that she was known as Brooke Shields's mother. It gave her a deep and personal validation. We were making it in the world. I think a part of Mom loved all of the attention because it was shared with me but was sadly often not articulate enough to get her point across the way she hoped.

She was trying to keep us talked-about and to make sure I was adored. She wanted to secure enough money to ensure us a substantial and comfortable future — something she never had as a kid. Mom wanted to make the best lives she could for us.

Whatever choices my mother made, positive or negative, they were what they were. She believed she was acting in my best interest always. And the cathexis I experienced rendered me immobile. It was so acute that I never questioned her judgment. Mom and I were symbiotically enmeshed and it would be years before I was able to see us as separate people.

My codependence was easily perpetuated because it felt familiar and I believed my mother knew the right way about everything. I was never given the space or the opportunity to make my own choices. I simply followed what she said and tried not to rock the boat. My priority was keeping my mother alive and that meant never leaving her. I believe I was primarily trying to protect my mother from herself and keep her from her own demise. It was an enormous distraction. I didn't have the time to focus on reviews, the trajectory of my career, boyfriends, or much else. Dating seemed almost silly. Plus, boys rarely asked me out because I was famous, and even though I was mature for my age, I was hardly experienced. I really only concerned myself with my studies and with my mother's well-being. I believed my mother held the key to my security in the world and my ticket to the future.

The main problem, though — aside from alcohol — was that Mom had no system of operations. She had no long-term plan except to gain financial security and keep my name out there. Her unconventional and often maddening approach to managing me solidified her lack of popularity within the entertainment business. She did not, however, seem to care or feel the need to adjust or justify her behavior. She also showed no signs of intending to ever ask for professional help. According to her, the system worked, and I lovingly agreed.

The Blue Lagoon remains the most successful movie I have ever made and the film with which I am the most identified. I'm serious when I say that a week rarely goes by in which *somebody* doesn't mention this movie to me. Generations have passed, and now those who watched the movie as teenagers are playing it for their children. For many it was their introduction to sex. Today, sex is introduced in a much more provocative and graphic way. Comparatively, *The Blue Lagoon* is mild. I still probably won't let my girls watch it. Too weird.

CHAPTER NINE:
THE BROOKE DOLL

Soon after I shot *The Blue Lagoon,* Mom bought a huge Tudor-style house in Englewood, New Jersey, right over the George Washington Bridge. The week before we moved into the house it was broken into and robbed. We suspected the interest in the stolen items stemmed from my being a recognizable name and the attention our move had gotten within the town. But *The Blue Lagoon* had not even been released yet and I was hardly famous in comparison to what I would soon become. Whatever the reason, a bunch of kids, conveniently led by the daughter of a local policeman, broke into the huge house and were caught walking out with rugs and other items.

The next day, Mom put the house back on the market, and since school had already started, we had little time to look for and move into a new home. I began an uncommon reverse commute from our New York

City apartment to my new high school campus. Mom still had our black Jeep Renegade, and I loved the ride in the mornings, going against commuter traffic as the sun was rising.

Mom kept up the search and eventually found another big Tudor-style home in a town called Haworth.

When we permanently left the apartment on Seventy-Third Street after almost fifteen years of living there, I wasn't sure whether I felt excited or apprehensive. It was probably a combination of both. I did love new starts and experiencing new lifestyles. But in the past, I had always been able to return to Manhattan. The drive to Haworth was only about forty-five minutes from the city, but it might as well have been a different country. I was not a Jersey girl. I was a native New Yorker through and through, and I felt my mom was the same. I knew that Mom always maintained her bond with New Jersey, but Newark was a far cry from the suburban town of Haworth and could not have been expected to quell her melancholy for her "homeland."

I began attending the Dwight-Englewood School in 1979. It was a shock to my system. Not only was I a new kid from Manhattan in a new high school in New

Jersey, but I was also suddenly taking classes with kids who had actually seen some of my movies. This was really the first time I was around peers who were aware of my celebrity. They were old enough to see movies like *Tilt* or *Just You and Me, Kid* and were very conscious of my fame.

To their credit, they were never unkind. I am sure that the school somehow made them aware that they should treat me just like a regular kid. It was a bit disconcerting, I'm sure, having a celebrity in your ninth-grade math class, but the kids seemed to be respectful of my space. They did so almost to a fault, however, because I ended up feeling set apart and lonesome. They were not being standoffish as much as reserved and slightly intimidated. Most of these kids had gone to the same grade school together and had become a tight-knit group that would take time to penetrate. The transition for me was going to require some effort.

My first term was pretty miserable and I was overwhelmed. The workload was unlike anything I had ever experienced. I had never seen so much homework and I had zero experience in navigating such a tough class schedule. Just navigating the vast campus to get to my classes on my own created a challenge. My grades were not great, I was living in isolated New Jersey, and I practically had no friends. I didn't mind the lack of friends, quite honestly, because I was fraught, awkward, and uncomfortable, and I wanted to hide. I dreaded getting out of the car each morning. Whenever I got the chance, I'd cry to my mother from the pay phone outside the science building. Mom kept reassuring me that it would all get better and that I had to just stick to it. She guaranteed me that I would soon make friends. I just had to keep holding my head up high.

My mom and I were getting along fine, and although I was concerned about her drinking, I was more concerned about her driving while drunk. We did not drive a lot in New York City, so it had never really been an issue, but now we were in need of a car for everything, and that created a new set of potential problems. For now, however, I had little time to dwell on her as much because I had to focus on getting my high school experience under control. How could I become integrated into this new school? How could I make friends?

Mom decided that I should invite my class to some party to help break the ice. There used to be a restaurant/club called Wednesdays in midtown that turned into a roller-skating rink one night a week. The owners offered to throw me a roller-skating Halloween party. All I had to do was take some photos and be seen enjoying the club. Mom told the owner that my entire class must be invited.

I sent out invitations and was terrified nobody would come. But as I was taking pictures for a few photographers, I saw a group of kids I recognized walk through the door. Soon the whole class was there and we were all dressed in Halloween costumes, rolling around to the music. It was so much fun and it turned out to be a perfect ice-breaker. I worried at first that maybe it felt like bribery and that I was buying the friendships. But it ended up being the social event that would show my peers that although I had lived an unusual life, I was, in fact, just a regular kid.

The best part about the whole thing was that the kids did not expect me to keep having parties and inviting them. They saw it as a bit of a job for me because I had to take photos with people and do interviews, and they realized that the party was in a way more for them and was in no way me showing off. From that night on, kids started slowly including me more and inviting me to study together or have sleepovers. I began to make friends all across the board. My closest friends were Lisa, Missy, Diane, and Gigi. All five of us remain friends to this day.

I tried to include my friends in my life whenever I could at photo shoots or events. Mom always made sure at least one of them accompanied me. When I worked with famous photographers like Francesco Scavullo or Bruce Weber, Mom always asked them to take a group shot of my friends and me. They always obliged, and my friends now have some pictures of themselves taken by some of the giants in art photography.

Mom loved joining my two worlds together. This was something I have never forgotten and have always appreciated. I kept inviting friends to events and parties. The events were actually work for me, so having a friend from my real life share it eased the burden. I also lived vicariously through their obvious enjoyment of the experiences. It was never the whole class again, but my close group of friends would get put on the list at places like the Red Parrot, Xenon, and sometimes Studio 54. Studio 54 was always easier to go to with just my mom because of the way the VIP area was set up. (How about that for a sentence? Ah, I was just a normal kid!)

By the time *The Blue Lagoon* was released and I had been labeled "The '80s Look" by *Time* magazine, I was already completely accepted by my new friends and they were unfazed by it all. High school can be a rough time for kids. Being a famous kid was not without its unique burdens, but I have always been thankful that my mom consistently forced us all to be accepting of the differences and not let my celebrity create a barrier. It was not easy, but she would not have it any other way. The press never gave Mom any recognition for this unique approach at all.

It was strange, too, that on the one hand Mom fought for my integration with kids my own age, yet on the other, she craved for me to become singled out and put on a pedestal by the world. This was a true contradiction — and some could say hypocritical — but it was the Teri way. I believe I managed to better regard my more grounded personal life because it was there that I felt unconditionally accepted. My mother constantly reinforced the importance of my life outside of work.

But the pressure was mounting in our public lives. During this time period, especially after *The Blue Lagoon* was such a hit, my professional life grew exponentially. It was all getting bigger and busier in many ways. Fans were now becoming a constant part of my life.

When it came to fan mail, Mom was incredibly diligent. I signed every autograph and honored every photo request, and Mom began by mailing each one out personally. It was getting to be too much, though, and we decided we needed help. My godmother, Auntie Lila, was working with us, and we had formed a corporation and named it Brooke Shields and Co. The "Co." soon grew to an office with two other women as staff members. One lady dealt with business requests and mail and the other with schedules. Mom soon hired another woman, who handled accounting and financial transactions. We had a handyman to help with the house and the office maintenance. We had lawyers, a money manager, a cleaning lady three days a week, and a part-time driver named Dick. We even hired a student to read through and categorize the letters.

There were the photo requests, people asking for advice, posters to be signed, as well as letters from "The Crazies." These were fans that raised a certain level of concern. They were basically stalkers who we handled differently than the honest fan